ESSENTIAL LAWS OF THE BOLIVIAN REVOLUTION

ESSENTIAL LAWS OF THE BOLIVIAN REVOLUTION

First Edition

A translation to English of the New Constitution; the Law Against Racism and any Form of Discrimination; and the Law Against Corruption, Illicit Enrichment and Investigation of Fortunes "Marcelo Quiroga Santa Cruz", of the Plurinational State of Bolivia.

By:

Luis Francisco Valle Velasco
Attorney at Law - Legal Translator
La Paz – Bolivia
www.vallevelasco.info

Cover photograph by: Patricio Crooker
www.patriciocrooker.com

ISBN-13: 978-1479204816
ISBN-10: 1479204811

CONTENTS

CONSTITUTION OF THE PLURINATIONAL STATE OF BOLIVIA

As published by the *Gaceta Oficial de Bolivia* on February, 2009.

INTRODUCTION

In immemorial times mountains arose, rivers were displaced, lakes were formed. Our Amazonia, our Chaco, our highlands and our plains and valleys were covered by greenness and flowers. We populated this sacred Mother Earth with different faces, and since then we understood the current plurality of all things and our diversity as beings and cultures. This is how we formed our towns, and we never understood racism until we suffered it in the terrible times of the colony.

The Bolivian people, of plural composition, since the profoundness of history, inspired in the battles of the past, in the indigenous anti-colonial uprising, in independence, in the popular liberation fights, in the indigenous, social and union marches, in the water and October wars, in the battles for land and territory, and with the memory of our martyrs, built a new State.

A State based in respect and equality among all, with principles of sovereignty, dignity, complementarity, solidarity, harmony and equity within the distribution and redistribution of the social product, with the predomination of the search to live well; with respect to the economic, social, legal, political and cultural plurality of the habitants of this land; in collective coexistence with access to water, work, education, health and household for everybody.

We left the colonial, republican and neoliberal State in the past. We assumed the historical challenge to collectively build a Social Unitary State of Plurinational Communitarian Law, which integrates and articulates the purposes of advancing towards a Bolivia that is democratic, productive, carrier and inspirer of peace, compromised with the integral development and with the free determination of its people.

We, men and women, through the Constitutional Assembly and with the originary power of the people, manifest our compromise with the unity and integrity of the country.

Complying with the mandate of our people, with the strength of our Pachamama and giving thanks to God, we refound Bolivia.

Honor and glory for the martyrs of this constituent and liberating feat that has made this new history possible.

EVO MORALES AYMA

CONSTITUTIONAL PRESIDENT OF BOLIVIA

Insofar as, the Bolivian People through the Referendum of January 25th of 2009, have approved the project of the State's Political Constitution, presented to the Honorable National Congress by the Constituent Assembly on December 15th of 2007 with the adjustments established by the Honorable National Congress. By the will of the sovereign the following is proclaimed:

POLITICAL CONSTITUTION OF THE STATE

FIRST PART

FUNDAMENTAL BASES OF THE STATE
RIGHTS, DUTIES AND GUARANTEES

TITLE I
FUNDAMENTAL BASES OF THE STATE

FIRST CHAPTER
MODEL OF THE STATE

Article 1. Bolivia is constituted in a Social Unitary State of Plurinational Communitarian Law, free, independent, sovereign, democratic, intercultural, decentralized and with autonomies. Bolivia is founded in plurality and in political, economic, legal, cultural and linguistic pluralism, within the integrating process of the country.

Article 2. Given the pre-colonial existence of the indigenous originary farmer nations and people and their ancestral domain over their territories, their free determination is guaranteed within the framework of the unity of the State, which consists in their right to autonomy, to self-government, to their culture, to the recognition of their institutions and to the consolidation of their territorial entities, in accordance to this Constitution and to the law.

Article 3. The Bolivian nation is formed by the totality of the Bolivian males and females, the indigenous originary farmer nations and people, and the intercultural and afro-Bolivian communities which altogether make up the Bolivian people.

Article 4. The State respects and guarantees freedom of religion and spiritual belief, according to their cosmovisions. The State is independent of religion.

Article 5.

I. The official languages of the State are the Spanish language and all of the languages of the indigenous originary farmer nations and people, that include the languages aymara, araona, naure, bésiro, canichana, cavineño, cayubaba, chácobo, chimán, ese ejia, guaraní, guarasu'we, guarayu, itonama, leco, machajuyai-kallawaya, machineri, maropa, mojeño-trinitario, mojeño-ignaciano, moré, mosetén, movima, pacawara, puquina, quechua, sirionó, tacana, tapiete, toromona, uru-chipaya, weenhayek, yaminawa, yuki, yuracaré and zamuco.

II. The plurinational Government and the departmental governments must use at least two of the official languages. One of them must be the Spanish language, and the other will be decided considering the use, convenience, circumstances, and needs and preferences of the total population or the territory in question. The rest of the autonomous governments must use the own languages of their territories, and one of them must be the Spanish language.

Article 6.

I. Sucre is the Capital of Bolivia.

II. The symbols of the State are the tricolor flag red, yellow and green; the Bolivian anthem; the coat of arms; the wiphala; the rosette; the kantuta flower and the patujú flower.

SECOND CHAPTER

PRINCIPLES, VALUES AND STATE PURPOSES

Article 7. Sovereignty resides in the Bolivian people, it is exercised in a direct and delegated manner. From it stems, by delegation, the functions and attributions of the organs of the public power; it is inalienable and imprescribable.

Article 8.

I. The State assumes and promotes as ethic-moral principles of the plural society: ama qhilla, ama llulla, ama suwa (don't be lazy, don't be a liar, don't be a thieve), suma qamaña (to live well), ñandereko (harmonious life), teko kavi (good life), ivi maraei (land without evil), and qhapaj ñan (noble path or life).

II. The State is supported in the values of unity, equality, inclusion, dignity, liberty, solidarity, reciprocity, respect, complementarity, harmony, transparency, balance, equality of opportunities, social and gender equity in participation, common well-being, responsibility, social justice, distribution and redistribution of the products and social assets, to live well.

Article 9. The following are the essential purposes and functions of the State, as well as the ones established by the Constitution and the law:

1. Constitute a just and harmonious society, founded in decolonization, without discrimination or exploitation, with plain social justice, to consolidate the plurinational identities.

2. Guarantee the well-being, the development, the security and the protection and equal dignity of the people, the nations, the towns and communities, and encourage mutual respect and intracultural, intercultural and plurilingual dialog.

3. Reaffirm and consolidate the unity of the country, and preserve its plurinational diversity as historical and human patrimony.

4. Guarantee the fulfillment of the principles, values, rights and duties recognized and established in this Constitution.

5. Guarantee the access of the people to education, health and labor.

6. Promote and guarantee the reasonable and planned use of the natural resources, and encourage their industrialization, through the development and strengthening of the productive base in its different dimensions and levels, as well as the conservation of the environment, for the well-being of current and future generations.

Article 10.

I. Bolivia is a pacifist State, which promotes the culture of peace and the right to peace, as well as the cooperation among peoples of the region and the world, in order to contribute to mutual knowledge, to equitable development and to the promotion of interculturality, with plain respect to the sovereignty of the states.

II. Bolivia rejects any war of aggression as an instrument of solution to differences and conflicts between states and it reserves the right to legitimate defense in case of aggression that compromises the independence and integrity of the State.

III.   The installation of foreign military bases within the Bolivian territory is prohibited.

THIRD CHAPTER

SYSTEM OF GOVERNMENT

Article 11.

I.   The Republic of Bolivia adopts for its government the democratic, participative, representative and communitarian form, with equivalence of conditions among males and females.

II.   Democracy is exercised in the following forms, which will all be developed by the law:

1.   Direct and participative, by means of the referendum, the citizens' legislative initiative, the revocation of mandate, the assembly, the town council and the prior consult. The assemblies and town councils will have a deliberative character according to Law.

2.   Representative, by means of the election of representatives by universal, direct and secret vote, according to Law.

3.   Communitarian, by means of the election, appointment or nomination of authorities and representatives by the own norms and procedures of the indigenous originary farmer nations and people, among others, according to Law.

Article 12.

I.   The State organizes and structures its public power through the Legislative, Executive, Judicial and Electoral organs. The organization of the State is founded on the independence, separation, coordination and cooperation among these organs.

II.   The control and defense of the society and the defense of the State are state functions.

III.   The functions of the public organs cannot be gathered in one sole organ nor can they be delegated among each other.

TITLE II

FUNDAMENTAL RIGHTS AND GUARANTEES

FIRST CHAPTER

GENERAL DISPOSITIONS

Article 13.

I. The rights recognized by this Constitution are inviolable, universal, interdependent, indivisible, and progressive. The State has the duty to promote, protect and respect them.

II. The rights proclaimed by this Constitution will not be understood as a negation of other non-enunciated rights.

III. The classification of rights established in this Constitution does not determine any hierarchy or superiority of some rights over others.

IV. The international treaties and agreements ratified by the Plurinational Legislative Assembly, which recognize human rights and that prohibit their limitation in States of Exception prevail in the internal order. The rights and duties established in this Constitution will be interpreted in accordance with international Treaties of human rights ratified by Bolivia.

Article 14.

I. All human beings have personality and legal capacity in accordance to the laws and enjoy the rights recognized by this Constitution, without any distinction.

II. The State prohibits and sanctions any form of discrimination founded on a reason of sex, color, age, sexual orientation, gender identity, origin, culture, nationality, citizenship, language, religious creed, ideology, political or philosophical affiliation, marital status, economic or social condition, type of occupation, grade of instruction, disability, pregnancy, or others that have as an objective or result in annulling or reducing the recognition, enjoyment and exercise, in conditions of equality, of the rights of every person.

III. The State guarantees to every person and collectivity, without any discrimination, the free and efficient exercise of the rights established in this Constitution, the laws and the international treaties of human rights.

IV.   While exercising their rights, nobody will be obligated to do what this Constitution and the laws don't mandate, or deprive themselves from what they don't prohibit.

V.   The Bolivian laws apply to every person, natural or legal, Bolivian or foreign, within the Bolivian territory.

VI.   Foreign males and females within the Bolivian territory have the rights and must comply with the duties established in this Constitution, apart from the restrictions contained herein.

SECOND CHAPTER

FUNDAMENTAL RIGHTS

Article 15.
I.   All persons have the right to life and to physical, psychological and sexual integrity. No one will be tortured, or will suffer cruel, inhumane, degrading and humiliating treatments. The death penalty does not exist.

II.   All persons, women in particular, have the right to not suffer physical, sexual or psychological violence, within the family and the society.

III.   The State will adopt the necessary measures to prevent, eliminate and sanction gender and generational violence, as well as any action or omission that has as its objective degrading the human condition, cause death, pain and physical, sexual and psychological suffering, within the public and private scope.

IV.   No person can be subjugated to forced disappearance for any cause or circumstance.

V.   No person can be subjugated to servitude or slavery. Human trafficking is prohibited.

Article 16.
I.   All persons have the right to water and food.

II.   The State has the obligation of guaranteeing food security, through a healthy, adequate and sufficient food provision for the entire population.

Article 17. All persons have the right to receive education in every level in a universal, productive, gratuitous, integral and intercultural manner, without distinction.

Article 18.

I.   All persons have the right to health.

II.   The State guarantees the inclusion and access to health to all persons, without exclusion or any discrimination.

III.   The unique health system will be universal, gratuitous, equitable, intracultural, intercultural, participative, with quality, warmness and social control.   The system is based in the principles of solidarity, efficiency and corresponsibility and is developed through public policies in every level of government.

Article 19.

I.   Every person has the right to a habitat or to adequate housing, which dignifies family and community life.

II.   The State, in every level of government, will promote social interest housing, through adequate financing systems, based in the principles of solidarity and equity.   These plans will be destined preferably to low resource families, to less favored groups and to the rural area.

Article 20.

I.   Every person has a universal and equitable right of access to basic services of potable water, sewage, electricity, home gas, mail and telecommunications.

II.   It is the responsibility of the State, in every level of government, the provision of the basic services through public, mixed, cooperative or communitary entities.   In the cases of electricity, home gas and telecommunications the services can be rendered by means of contracts with private companies.   The provision of services must respond to the criteria of responsibility, accessibility, continuity, quality, efficiency, effectiveness, equitable tariffs and necessary coverage: with participation and social control.

III.   The access to water and sewage constitute human rights, they will not be granted in concessions or be privatized and they are subjected to the licenses and registrations regime, in accordance to law.

THIRD CHAPTER

CIVIL AND POLITICAL RIGHTS

SECTION I

CIVIL RIGHTS

Article 21. Bolivian males and females have the following rights:

1. To cultural self-identification.

2. To privacy, intimacy, respect, honor, own image and dignity.

3. To freedom of thought, spirituality, religion and cult, expressed in an individual or collective manner, in public as well as in private, for licit purposes.

4. To freedom of gathering and association, in a public or private manner, for licit purposes.

5. To freely express and spread thoughts or opinions by any means of communication, in an oral, written or visual manner, individually or collectively.

6. To access information, interpreting, analyzing and communicating it freely, individually or collectively.

7. To freedom of residence, stay and circulation within all of the Bolivian territory, that includes the entrance and exit to and from the country.

Article 22. The dignity and freedom of the person are inviolable. Respecting and protecting them is the fundamental duty of the State.

Article 23.

I. Every person has the right to freedom and personal security. Personal liberty can only be restricted within the limits set forth by law, in order to assure the discovery of the historic truth within the intervention of the jurisdictional instances.

II. The imposition of freedom-depriving measures to adolescents will be avoided. Every adolescent that is deprived of liberty will receive preferable attention by the judicial, administrative and law enforcing authorities. These shall assure at every moment the respect to its dignity and the reserve of its identity. The detention shall be completed in different facilities than those assigned for adults, taking into account the own needs of its age.

III. No one can be detained, apprehended, or deprived from freedom, unless in the cases and in accordance to the ways established by law. The execution of the order will require that it be issued by a competent authority and that it be in writing.

IV.   Any person found in the flagrant commission of a crime can be apprehended by any person, even without an order. The sole objective of the apprehension will be to conduct the individual before judicial authority, who shall resolve the legal situation of the person within a maximum term of twenty-four hours.

V.   At the moment when a person is deprived from its freedom, it will be informed of the motives for its detention, as well as of the accusation or criminal complaint formulated against it.

VI.   The responsible of the reclusion centers shall carry a registry of persons deprived from freedom. They will not receive any person without copying in this registry the corresponding order. Its non-compliance will result in the prosecution and sanctions established by law.

Article 24. Every person has the individual or collective right to petition, in an oral or written manner, and to obtain a formal and prompt response. In order to exercise this right there will not be any other requirement than the petitioner's identification.

Article 25.

I.   Every person has the right to inviolability of domicile and to secrecy in private communications in all of its forms, unless judicial authorization.

II.   Correspondence, private papers and private manifestations contained in any support are inviolable, they cannot be seized unless in the cases determined by law for penal investigation, in virtue of written order and motivated by judicial competent authority.

III.   Neither public authority, nor any person or entity can intercept private conversations or communications through an installation to control or centralize them.

IV.   The information and evidence obtained by violating correspondence and communications in any of its forms will not produce legal effect.

SECTION II

POLITICAL RIGHTS

Article 26.

I.   All of the male and female citizens have the right to freely participate in the formation, exercise and control of the political power, directly or by means of representatives, individually or collectively. The participation will be equitable and in equality of conditions among men and women.

II.   The right of participation includes:

1.   Organization for purposes of political participation, in accordance to the Constitution and the laws.

2.   Suffrage, through equal, universal, direct, individual, secret, free and obligatory vote, publicly counted. Suffrage will be exercised after turning age eighteen.

3.   Where communitarian democracy is practiced, the electoral processes will be exercised according to their own norms and procedures, supervised by the Electoral Organ, as long as the electoral act is not subjected to equal, universal, direct, individual, secret, free and obligatory vote.

4.   The election, appointment and direct nomination of the representatives of the indigenous originary farmer nations and people, in accordance with their own norms and procedures.

5.   The fiscalization of the acts of the public function.

Article 27.

I.   Bolivian males and females who reside abroad have the right to participate in the elections for President and Vice-president of the State, and in the others specified by law. The right will be exercised through a voter registration conducted by the Electoral Organ.

II.   Foreign males and females residing in Bolivian have the right to suffrage in municipal elections, in accordance to law, applying the principles of international reciprocity.

Article 28. The exercise of political rights is suspended in the following cases, after an executory sentence and while the penalty has not been fulfilled:

1.   For taking arms and rendering services for enemy armed forces in times of war.

2.   For defrauding public resources.

3.   For treason to the country.

Article 29.

I. The right to request and receive asylum and refugee status due to political and ideological prosecution for foreign males and females is recognized, in accordance with the laws and international treaties.

II. Any person to whom asylum or refuge is granted in Bolivia shall not be expelled or delivered to a country where its life, integrity, security or freedom may be in danger. The State will assist in a positive, humanitarian and expedite manner the requests of family reunification presented by parents or children with an asylum or refugee status.

CHAPTER FOUR

RIGHTS OF THE INDIGENOUS ORIGINARY FARMER NATIONS AND PEOPLE

Article 30.

I. The indigenous originary farmer nations and people constitute the human collective groups that share cultural identity, language, historical tradition, institutions, territoriality, and cosmovisions, with an existence prior to the Spanish colonial invasion.

II. Within the framework of the State's unity and in accordance with this Constitution the indigenous originary farmer nations and people enjoy the following rights:

1. To exist freely.

2. To their cultural identity, religious creed, spiritualties, practices and customs, and to their own cosmovision.

3. To have the cultural identity of each of its members, if wanted, be registered alongside the Bolivian citizenship in its identity document, passport or other identification document with legal validity.

4. To free determination and territoriality.

5. To have their institutions be part of the general structure of the State.

6. To the collective titling of lands and territories.

7. To the protection of their sacred places.

8.   To create and manage their own systems, mediums and networks of communication.

9.   To have their traditional knowledge and intelligence, their traditional medicine, their languages, their rituals and their symbols and clothing valued, respected and promoted.

10.   To live in a healthy environment, with an adequate handling and use of the ecosystems.

11.   To the collective intellectual property of their intelligence, sciences and knowledge, as well as their valuation, use, promotion and development.

12.   To an intracultural, intercultural and plurilingual education in all of the educational system.

13.   To the universal and gratuitous health system that respects its cosmovision and traditional practices.

14.   To the exercise of their political, legal and economic systems according to their cosmovisions.

15.   To be consulted by means of the appropriate procedures, and in particular through their institutions, every time legislative or administrative measures susceptible of affecting them are anticipated. Within this framework, the right to an obligatory prior consultation will be respected and guaranteed, conducted by the State, in good faith and in an agreed manner, regarding the exploitation of non-renewable natural resources within the territory where they are located.

16.   To a participation of the benefits resulting from the exploitation of natural resources in their territories.

17.   To indigenous autonomous territory administration, and to the use and exclusive management of the renewable natural resources existent in their territories without prejudice of the rights legitimately acquired by third persons.

18.   To participation in the organs and institutions of the State.

III.   The State guarantees, respects and protects the rights of the indigenous originary farmer nations and people established in this Constitution and in the law.

Article 31.

I.   The indigenous originary nations and people in danger of extinction, in situation of voluntary isolation and not contacted, will be protected and respected in their individual and collective ways of life.

II.   The indigenous originary nations and people in isolation and not contacted enjoy the right to maintain that condition, to the delimitation and legal consolidation of the territory they occupy and live in.

Article 32. The afro-Bolivian people enjoy, in everything it corresponds, the economic, social, political and cultural rights recognized in the Constitution for the indigenous originary farmer nations and people.

CHAPTER FIVE

SOCIAL AND ECONOMIC RIGHTS

SECTION I

RIGHT TO THE ENVIRONMENT

Article 33. All persons have the right to a healthy, protected and balanced environment. The exercise of this right must allow individuals and collectivities of current and future generations, as well as other living beings, to develop in a normal and permanent manner.

Article 34. Any person, individually or representing a collectivity, is authorized to exercise the legal actions in defense of the right to the environment, without prejudice of the obligation of the public institutions of acting ex officio against the attacks to the environment.

SECTION II

RIGHT TO HEALTH AND SOCIAL SECURITY

Article 35.

I.   The State, in all of its levels, will protect the right to health, promoting public policies oriented to improving the quality of life, the collective wellbeing and the gratuitous access of the population to health services.

II.   The health system is unique and it includes the traditional medicine of the indigenous originary farmer nations and people.

Article 36.
I.   The State will guarantee the access to universal health insurance.

II.   The State will control the exercise of the public and private health services, and will regulate it through law.

Article 37. The State has the undeniable obligation of guaranteeing and sustaining the right to health, which is a supreme function and a prime financial responsibility. Both health promotion and the prevention of deceases will be prioritized.

Article 38.
I.   Public goods and services related to health are property of the State, and cannot be privatized or given in concessions.

II.   Health services will be rendered in an uninterrupted manner.

Article 39.
I.   The State will guarantee public health services and recognizes private health services; will regulate and supervise the attention to quality through sustainable medical audits that evaluate the work of the personnel, the infrastructure and the equipment, in accordance to law.

II.   The law will sanction negligent actions or omissions in the exercise of the medical practice.

Article 40. The State will guarantee the participation of the organized population within decision making, and within the administration of the entire public health system.

Article 41.
I.   The State guarantees the access of the population to medicines.

II.   The State will prioritize generic medicines through the encouragement of their domestic production and, in its case, will determine its import.

III.   The right of access to medicines cannot be restricted by intellectual property and trade rights, and will contemplate standards of quality and first generation.

Article 42.
I.   It is the responsibility of the State to promote and guarantee the respect, use, investigation and practice of traditional medicine, recovering the

ancestral knowledge and practices starting from the thoughts and values of all of the indigenous originary farmer nations and people.

II. The promotion of traditional medicine will incorporate the registration of natural medicines and their active principles, as well the protection of its knowledge as intellectual, historic, and cultural property, and as the patrimony of the indigenous originary farmer nations and people.

III. The law will regulate the exercise of traditional medicine and will guarantee the quality of its service.

Article 43. The law will regulate cell, tissue or organ donations or transplants under the principles of humanity, solidarity, opportunity, gratuity and efficiency.

Article 44.
I. No person will be subjected to a surgical intervention, medical or laboratory examination without its consent or from legally authorized third persons, unless imminent danger to its life.

II. No person will be subjected to scientific experiments without its consent.

Article 45.
I. All of the Bolivian males and females have the right of access to social security.

II. Social security is rendered under the principles of universality, integrality, equity, solidarity, unity of administration, economy, opportunity, interculturality, and efficacy. Its direction and administration corresponds to the State, with social control and participation.

III. The social security regime covers attention due to sickness, epidemic, and catastrophic diseases; maternity and paternity; professional and labor risks and risks due to field work; disability and special needs; unemployment and loss of job; orphanhood, incapacity, widowhood, old age, and death; housing, family assistance and other social previsions.

IV. The State guarantees the right to retirement, with universal, supportive, and equitable characteristics.

V. Women have the right to a safe maternity, with an intercultural vision and practice; will enjoy special assistance and the protection of the State during pregnancy, delivery and during the pre-natal or post-natal periods.

VI. The public social security services cannot be privatized or given in concessions.

SECTION III

RIGHT TO WORK AND EMPLOYMENT

Article 46.

I.   Every person has the right to:

1. To a dignified job, with industrial security, hygiene and occupational health, without discrimination, and with a just, equitable and satisfactory wage or salary, that assures a dignified existence for the person and its family.

2. To a stable workplace, in equitable and satisfactory conditions.

II.   The state will protect the conduction of work activities in all of its forms.

III.   All kinds of forced labor or other type of analog ways of exploitation that obliges a person to work without its consent and just retribution is prohibited.

Article 47.

I.   Every person has the right to engage in commerce, industry or in any licit economic activity, in conditions that are not detrimental to the collective good.

II.   The working males and females of small urban and rural productive units, self-employed, and trade unionists in general, will enjoy from the State a special protection regime, through a policy of equitable commercial trade and just prices for their products, as well as the preferential assignation of economic financial resources to give an incentive to their production.

III.   The State will protect, encourage and strengthen the communitarian ways of production.

Article 48.

I.   The social and labor provisions are of mandatory compliance.

II.   Labor norms will be interpreted and applied under the principles of protection of the working males and females as the main productive force of society; of primacy of the labor relation; of labor continuity and stability; of no discrimination and of transfer of the burden of proof in favor of the working man or woman.

III.   The rights and benefits recognized in favor or the working males and females cannot be waived, and all the conventions contrary to or that tend to evade its effects are null.

IV.   The accrued salaries or wages, labor rights, social benefits and contributions to social security not paid have privilege and preference over any other amount due, and are unseizable and imprescribable.

V.   The State will promote the incorporation of women to the labor force and will guarantee for them the same wages that men receive for a job of equal value, in both the public and private environments.

VI.   Women con not be discriminated or fired due to their marital status, pregnancy situation, age, physical characteristics or number of children. Job tenure is guaranteed for pregnant women, and for the father, until the son or daughter is one year of age.

VII.   The State will guarantee the incorporation of male and female teenagers in the productive system, in accordance to their training and formation.

Article 49.

I.   The right to collective negotiation is recognized.

II.   The law will regulate the labor relations relative to contracts and collective agreements; general and specific minimum wages and salary increases; reincorporation; paid rest periods and holidays; counting of seniority; work day, extra hours, night payment, Sunday payment; year-end bonus, bonuses and other systems of participation in the profits of the company; indemnities and severance payments; labor maternity; training and professional formation, and other social rights.

III.   The State will protect labor stability. Unjustified dismissal and any type of labor harassment are prohibited. The law will determine the corresponding sanctions.

Article 50.   The State, through specialized administrative courts and organisms, will resolve the conflicts emerging from labor relations between employers and employees, included those of industrial security and of social security.

Article 51.

I.   All of the working males and females have the right to organize themselves in unions in accordance to law.

II.   The State will respect union principles, union democracy, political pluralism, self-sustainability, solidarity and internationalism.

III.   Unionization is recognized and guaranteed as a medium of defense, representation, assistance, education and culture of the working males and females of the countryside and of the city.

IV.   The State will respect the ideological and organizational independence of the unions. The unions will enjoy legal personality for the sole fact of being organized and recognized by their parent entities.

V.   The tangible and intangible patrimony of union organizations is inviolable, unseizable and undelegable.

VI.   The union male and female leaders enjoy the right to employment security for union representatives, they cannot be dismissed until a year after the ending of their administration and their social rights cannot be reduced, nor will they be subjected to prosecution or incarceration for acts conducted while performing their union duties.

Article 52.
I.   The right to free business association is recognized and guaranteed.

II.   The State guarantees the acknowledgement of the legal personality of business associations, as well as of the democratic organizational business forms, in accordance to their own by-laws.

III.   The State recognizes the training institutions of business organizations.

IV.   The patrimony of business organizations, tangible and intangible, is inviolable and unseizable.

Article 53. The right to labor strike is guaranteed as the exercise of the legal faculty of the working males and females to suspend labor for the defense of their rights, in accordance to law.

Article 54.
I.   It is the obligation of the State to establish employment policies to avoid unemployment and suboccupation, with the goal of creating, maintaining and generating conditions that guarantee possibilities for occupational labor and a just retribution for male and female workers.

II.   It is the duty of the State and of society the protection and defense of the industrial apparatus and of state services.

III.   Male and female workers, in defense of their work places and in protection of the social interest can, in accordance to law, reactivate and reorganize companies in processes of bankruptcy, insolvency or liquidation, closed or abandoned in an unjustified manner, forming communitarian or social companies. The State can contribute to the action taken by male and female workers.

Article 55. The cooperative system is sustained in the principles of solidarity, equality, reciprocity, equity of distribution, social purpose, and no profit for its associates. The State will encourage and regulate the organization of cooperatives through law.

SECTION IV

RIGHT TO PROPERTY

Article 56.

I.   Every person has the right to individual or collective private property, as long as it performs a social function.

II.   Private property is guaranteed as long as its use is not detrimental to the collective interest.

III.   The right to succession by inheritance is guaranteed.

Article 57. Expropriation will be imposed in case of need, public benefit or good, qualified in accordance to law and prior receiving a just indemnity. Urban real estate property is not subjected to reversion.

SECTION V

RIGHT TO CHILDHOOD, YOUTH AND ADOLESCENCE

Article 58. A girl, a boy or an adolescent are considered to be persons who are minors of age. Girls, boys and adolescents are entitled to enjoy the rights recognized in the Constitution, within the limits established herein, and the specific rights inherent to their development process; to their ethnic, socio-cultural, gender, and generational identity; and to the satisfaction of their needs, interests and aspirations.

Article 59.

I.   Every girl, boy or adolescent has the right to an integral development.

II.   Every girl, boy or adolescent has the right to live and grow within the core of its original or adoptive family. When this is not possible, or it's contrary to its superior interest, will have the right to a substitute family, in accordance to law.

III.   Every girl, boy or adolescent, without distinction due to origin, enjoys equality of rights and duties with regards to their parents. Discrimination by parents towards their children will be sanctioned by law.

IV.   Every girl, boy or adolescent has the right to an identity and to registration with regards to its parents. When the parents are not known, the last name used will be chosen by the person responsible of its care.

V.   The State and the society will guarantee the protection, promotion and active participation of male and female youth within the productive, political, social, economic and cultural development, without any discrimination, in accordance to law.

Article 60. It is the duty of the State, of society and of the family to guarantee the priority of the superior interest of the girl, boy and adolescent, that comprises the preeminence of its rights, the primacy in receiving protection and aid in any circumstance, the priority of attention of the public and private services, and the access to an administration of justice that is fast, timely and with specialized personal assistance.

Article 61.

I.   Any kind of violence towards girls, boy or adolescents, within the family or within the society, is prohibited and will be sanctioned.

II.   Forced labor and children exploitation are prohibited. The activities conducted by girls, boys or adolescents within the family and society will be oriented to their integral formation as female and male citizens, having a formative function. Their rights, guarantees and institutional mechanisms of protection will be set forth in a special regulation.

SECTION VI

RIGHTS OF FAMILIES

Article 62. The State recognizes and protects families as the fundamental core of society, and will guarantee the social and economic conditions for its integral development. All of its members have equal rights, duties and opportunities.

Article 63.

I.   The marriage between woman and man is constituted by legal bonds and it's based in the equality of rights and duties of the spouses.

II.   Free unions or unions of fact that meet conditions of stability and singularity, maintained by a woman and a man without legal impediment, will produce the same effects as the civil marriage, in what concerns the personal and patrimonial relations of the of the co-habitants as well as in what relates to their adopted or procreated male and female children.

Article 64.

I.   Spouses or co-habitants have the duty of attending, in equality of conditions and through common effort, the support and responsibility of the home, the education and integral formation of the male and female children when these are minors or have a disability.

II.   The State will protect and assist those who are responsible of the families in exercise of their obligations.

Article 65. In virtue of the superior interest of the girls, boys and adolescents and their right to an identity, the presumption of affiliation will be valid by indication of the mother or the father. This presumption will be valid unless there is conflicting evidence presented by whoever denies the affiliation. In case there is evidence that denies the presumption, the incurred costs will correspond to whoever indicated the affiliation.

Article 66. Women and men are guaranteed the exercise of their sexual rights and their reproductive rights.

SECTION VII

RIGHTS OF SENIOR CITIZENS

Article 67.

I.   Aside for the rights recognized in this Constitution, all senior citizens have the right to live their old ages with dignity, human quality and warmness.

II.   The State will promote a life annuity for senior citizens within the framework of the integral social security system, in accordance to law.

Article 68.

I.   The State will adopt public policies for the protection, attention, recreation, rest and social occupation of senior citizens, in accordance to their capabilities and possibilities.

II.   Any form of mistreatment, abandonment, violence and discrimination against senior citizens is prohibited and will be sanctioned.

Article 69. The Veterans of the Country deserve gratitude and respect from public and private institutions and from the general population, they will be considered heroes and defenders of Bolivia and will receive from the State a life pension, in accordance to law.

SECTION VIII

RIGHTS OF PERSONS WITH DISABILITIES

Article 70. Any person with a disability enjoys the following rights:

1.   To be protected by its family and by the State.

2.   To integral and gratuitous education and health.

3.   To communication in alternative language.

4.   To work in adequate conditions, according to its possibilities and capabilities, with a just remuneration that assures a dignified life.

5.   To the development of its individual potentials.

Article 71.

I.   Any type of discrimination, mistreatment, violence and exploitation towards a person with a disability is prohibited and will be sanctioned.

II.   The State will adopt positive action measures to promote the effective integration of the persons with disabilities within the productive, economic, political, social and cultural sectors, without any discrimination.

III. The State will generate the conditions that allow the development of the individual potentials of the persons with disabilities.

Article 72. The State will guarantee the integral services of prevention and rehabilitation of the persons with disabilities, as well as other benefits established by law.

SECTION IX

RIGHTS OF PERSONS DEPRIVED OF LIBERTY

Article 73.

I.   Any person subjected to any form of liberty deprivation will be treated with the due respect to human dignity.

II.   All persons deprived of liberty have the right to communicate freely with their defenders, interpreters, family members and related individuals. The lack of communication is prohibited. Any limitation of communication can only proceed within the framework of the investigations conducted for the commission of a crime, and will only last for a maximum term of 24 hours.

Article 74.

I.   The State is responsible for the social reinsertion of the persons deprived of liberty, for making sure their rights are respected, and for their retention and custody in adequate places, in accordance to the classification, nature and graveness of the crime, as well as the age and sex of the detained individuals.

II.   The persons deprived of liberty will have the opportunity to work and study inside penitentiary centers.

SECTION X

RIGHTS OF MALE AND FEMALE USERS AND CONSUMERS

Article 75. The male and female users and consumers enjoy the following rights:

    1.   To the provision of food, medicines and products in general, in conditions of harmlessness, quality, and adequate and sufficient

available quantity, with an efficient and timely provisions of supplies.

2. To trustworthy information about the characteristics and contents of the products they consume and services they use.

Article 76.

I. The State guarantees the access to an integral transportation system in its diverse modalities. The law will determine that the transportation system be efficient and effective, and that it generates benefits to the users and providers.

II. There cannot be any customs controls, stations or control posts of any nature within the Bolivian territory, with the exception of those created by law.

CHAPTER SIX

EDUCATION, INTERCULTURALITY AND CULTURAL RIGHTS

SECTION I

EDUCATION

Article 77.

I. Education is a supreme function and a prime financial responsibility of the State, who has the undeniable obligation to sustain, guarantee and administer it.

II. The State and society have full tuition over the educational system, which comprises regular, alternative and special education, and superior education of professional formation. The educational system develops its processes based in the criterion of harmony and coordination.

III. The educational system is made up of fiscal educational institutions, private educational institutions and of agreement.

Article 78.

I. Education is unitary, public, universal, democratic, participative, communitarian, decolonizing and of quality.

II. Education is intracultural, intercultural and plurilingual within the entire educational system.

III.   The educational system is founded in education that is open, humanist, scientific, technical and technological, productive, territorial, theoretical and practical, liberating and revolutionary, critical and supportive

IV.   The State guarantees vocational education and humanist technical teaching, for men and women, related to life, work and productive development.

Article 79.   Education will foster patriotism, intercultural dialog and moral ethical values. The values will incorporate gender equity, no difference in roles, no violence and the enforcement of human rights.

Article 80.
I.   Education will have as its objective the integral formation of the people and the strengthening of critical social conscience in life and for life. Education will be oriented towards individual and collective formation; to the development of capabilities, aptitudes and physical and intellectual abilities that link theory with productive practice; to the conservation and protection of the environment, biodiversity and territory in order to live well. Its regulation and performance will be established by law.

II.   Education will contribute to strengthening the unity and identity of all persons as part of the Plurinational State, as well as the identity and cultural development of the members of each indigenous originary farmer nation or town, and the intercultural understanding and enrichment within the State.

Article 81.
I.   Education is mandatory until graduation from high school.

II.   Fiscal education is free in all of its levels until the superior.

III.   When finishing high school studies the Bachelor Diploma will be given to the student, in a gratuitous and immediate manner.

Article 82.
I.   The State guarantees the access to education and the permanency of all the male and female citizens in conditions of full equality.

II.   The State will support with priority the students with less economic possibilities to access the different levels of the educational system, through economic resources, food programs, clothing, transportation, school material; and in scattered areas, with student residences, in accordance to law.

III.   Scholarships will be given to students who achieve excellent results in all of the levels of the educational system. All girls, boys and adolescents with outstanding natural talent have the right to be educationally attended with formation and learning methods that allow the achievement of the greatest development of their aptitudes and skills.

Article 83. Social participation, communitarian participation and that of the parents within the educational system are recognized and guaranteed, through representative organisms in all levels of the State and in the indigenous originary farmer nations and people. Its compositions and attributions will be established by law.

Article 84. The State and society have the duty of eradicating illiteracy through programs that go in tune with the cultural and linguistic reality of the population.

Article 85. The State will promote and guarantee permanent education for girls, boys and adolescents with disabilities, or with extraordinary talents in learning, under the same structure, principles and values of the educational system, and will establish special curricular organizations and development.

Article 86. Educational centers will recognize and guarantee freedom of conscience, faith and religious teachings, as well as the spirituality of the indigenous originary farmer nations and people, and will foster respect and mutual co-habitation among people of diverse religious options, without dogmatic imposition. The religious option of any male and female student will not be reason to discriminate their acceptance and permanency in these centers.

Article 87. The operation of educational units of agreement with social service objectives, free access and no profit generating purposes is recognized and respected, which shall function under the supervision of public authorities, respecting the right of administration of religious entities over such academic units, without prejudice of what is established in national provisions, and will be ruled by the same norms, policies, plans and programs of the educational system.

Article 88.

I.   The operation of private educational units in all levels and modalities is recognized and respected; they will be ruled by the policies, plans, programs and authorities of the educational system. The State guarantees their operation prior verifying their conditions and compliance with the requisites established by law.

II.   The right of the mother and the father to choose the best suited education for their sons and daughters is respected.

Article 89. The follow-up, measurement, evaluation and accreditation of the educational quality in the entire educational system, will be in charge of a public, technically specialized institution independent from the Ministry of the area. Its composition and operation will be determined by law.

Article 90.

I. The State recognizes the validity of institutes of humanistic, technical and technological formation, in the medium and superior levels, prior complying with the conditions and requisites established by law.

II. The State will promote technical, technological, productive, artistic and linguistic formation, through technical institutes.

III. The State, through the educational system, will promote the creation and organization of remote learning and of popular but not scholarized educational programs, with the objective of elevating the cultural level and developing the plurinational conscience of the people.

SECTION II

SUPERIOR EDUCATION

Article 91.

I. Superior education develops the professional formation processes, of generation and revelation of knowledge oriented towards the integral development of society, for which takes into account universal knowledge and collective understanding of the indigenous originary farmer nations and people.

II. Superior education is intracultural, intercultural and plurilingual, and has as its mission the integral formation of the human resources with high qualification and professional competency; the development of scientific investigation processes to resolve the problems of the productive base and its social surroundings; the promotion of extension and social interaction policies to strengthen the scientific, cultural and linguistic diversity; the participation alongside the people within the processes of social liberation, to construct a society with more equity and social justice.

III. Superior education comprises universities, superior schools of formation in teaching, and technical, technological and artistic institutes, fiscal or private.

Article 92.

I.   Public universities are autonomous and equal in hierarchy. The autonomy consists in the free administration of their resources; the appointment of their authorities, its teaching and administrative personnel; the elaboration and approval of their by-laws, study plans and yearly budgets; and the acceptance of bequests and donations, as well as the subscription of contracts, to achieve their objectives and sustain and perfect their institutes and faculties. Public universities can negotiate loans using their properties and resources as guarantee, prior a legislative approval.

II.   Public universities will constitute, while in exercise of their autonomy, the Bolivian University, which will coordinate and schedule its objectives and functions through a central organism, according to the university development plan.

III.   Public universities will be authorized to extend academic diplomas and professional degrees that are valid throughout the entire State.

Article 93.

I.   Public universities will be mandatorily and sufficiently subsidized by the State, independently from departmental, municipal and their own resources, created or to be created.

II.   Public universities, within the framework of their by-laws, will establish social participation mechanisms of advice, coordination and consulting character.

III.   Public universities will establish mechanisms of accountability and transparency in the use of their resources, through the presentation of financial statements to the Plurinational Legislative Assembly, the General Controller and the Executive Organ.

IV.   Public universities, within the framework of their by-laws, will establish academic and intercultural dispersal programs, according to the necessities of the State and of the indigenous originary farmer nations and people.

V.   The State, in coordination with public universities, will promote in the rural areas the creation and operation of universities and pluricultural communitarian institutes, assuring social participation. The opening and operation of such universities will respond to the productive strengthening needs of the region, considering its potentials.

Article 94.

I.   Private universities will be ruled by the policies, plans, programs and authorities of the educational system. Their operation will be authorized by means of a supreme decree, prior verifying their compliance with the conditions and requisites established by law.

II.   Private universities will be authorized to issue academic diplomas. Professional degrees that are valid throughout the country will be issued by the State.

III.   In private universities, in order to obtain an academic diploma in any of the university graduation modalities, an examining court will be constituted, which will be integrated by professors, appointed by the public universities, in the conditions established by law. The State will not subsidize private universities.

Article 95.

I.   The universities will have to create and sustain intercultural centers of formation and technical and cultural training, of free access to the people, in agreement with the principles and objectives of the educational system.

II.   The universities will have to implement programs for the recovery, preservation, development, learning and disclosure of the different languages of the indigenous originary farmer nations and people.

III.   The universities will promote centers for the generation of productive units, in coordination with communitarian productive initiatives, public and private.

Article 96.

I.   It is the responsibility of the State to form and train teachers for public teaching, through superior formation schools. The formation of teachers will be unique, fiscal, gratuitous, intracultural, intercultural, plurilingual, scientific and productive, and will be developed with social compromise and vocation towards service.

II.   The teachers of the sector will have to participate in continuous update and pedagogic training processes.

III.   The teaching career and job security of the teachers of the sector is guaranteed, in accordance to law. The teachers will enjoy a dignified salary.

Article 97. Post-gradual formation in all of its levels will have as its fundamental mission the qualification of professionals in different areas, through scientific investigation processes and the generation of knowledge linked with reality, to contribute to the integral development of society. Post-gradual formation will be coordinated by an instance formed by the universities of the educational system, in accordance to law.

SECTION III

CULTURES

Article 98.

I.   Cultural diversity forms part of the essential foundation of the Plurinational Communitarian State. Interculturality is the instrument of cohesion and harmonious and balanced conviviality amongst all peoples and nations. Interculturality will respect differences within equal conditions.

II.   The State assumes the existence of originary indigenous farmer cultures as reservoirs of values, knowledge, spirituality and cosmovisions.

III.   It will be the fundamental responsibility of the State to preserve, develop, protect and promote the cultures existent in the country.

Article 99.

I.   The cultural patrimony of the Bolivian people is inalienable, unseizable and imprescribable. The economic resources generated therefrom will be regulated by law, to attend its conservation, preservation and promotion with the outmost priority.

II.   The State will guarantee the registration, protection, restoration, recuperation, revitalization, enrichment, promotion and spreading of its cultural patrimony, in accordance to law.

III.   The natural, arqueological, paleontological, historic, documentary, from religious cult and folkloric wealth, forms part of the cultural patrimony of the Bolivian people, in accordance to law.

Article 100.

I.   It is the patrimony of the indigenous originary farmer nations and peoples the cosmovisions, the myths, the oral history, the dances, the cultural practices, the knowledge and traditional technologies. This patrimony forms part of the expression and identity of the State.

II.   The State will protect the learning and knowledge by means of the corresponding intellectual property registration that safeguards the intangible rights of the indigenous originary farmer nations and people and the intercultural and afro-Bolivian communities.

Article 101. Manifestations of art and popular industries, in their intangible component, will enjoy special protection from the State. Likewise, this protection applies to places and activities declared as cultural patrimony of humanity, in their tangible and intangible components.

Article 102. The State will register and protect the intellectual, individual and collective property of the works and discoveries of authors, artists, composers, inventors and scientists, in the conditions determined by law.

SECTION IV

SCIENCE, TECHNOLOGY AND INVESTIGATION

Article 103.

I.   The State will guarantee the development of scientific, technical and technological science and investigation in benefit of the general interest. The necessary resources will be provided and a state science and technology system will be created.

II.   The State will have the policy of implementing strategies to incorporate the knowledge and application of new information and communication technologies.

III.   The State, the universities, the public and private productive service companies, and the indigenous originary farmer nations and people, will develop and coordinate investigation, innovation, promotion, revelation, application and transfer of science and technology processes to strengthen the productive base and encourage the integral development of society, in accordance to law.

SECTION V

SPORTS AND RECREATION

Article 104. Every person has the right to sports, to physical culture and to recreation. The State guarantees the access to sports without distinction of gender, language, religion, political orientation, territorial location, and social, cultural or any other kind of belonging.

Article 105. The State will promote, through education policies, recreation and public health, the development of physical culture and the practice of sports in its preventive, recreational, formative and competitive levels, with special attention to people with disabilities. The State will guarantee the mediums and economic resources necessary for its effectiveness.

CHAPTER SEVEN

SOCIAL COMMUNICATION

Article 106.

I.   The State guarantees the right to communication and the right to information.

II.   The State guarantees to Bolivian males and females the right of freedom of expression, opinion and information, to rectification and reply, and the right to freely express ideas through any broadcasting medium, without prior censorship.

III. The State guarantees to the male and female workers of the press freedom of expression and the right to communication and information.

IV.   The conscience clause of the workers of information is recognized.

Article 107.

I.   Social communication mediums shall contribute to the promotion of the ethical, moral and patriotic values of the different cultures of the country, with the production and broadcasting of plurilingual educational programs and in an alternative language for the disabled.

II.   The information and opinions delivered through social communication mediums shall respect the principles of veracity and responsibility. These principles will be exercised through the ethics and self-regulation norms of the organizations of the press and mediums of communication and their law.

III. Social communication mediums cannot form, directly or indirectly, monopolies or oligopolies.

IV.   The State will support the creation of communitarian communication mediums in equality of conditions and opportunities.

TITLE III

DUTIES

Article 108. The following are the duties of Bolivian males and females:

1. To know, abide and uphold the Constitution.

2. To know, respect and promote the rights recognized in the Constitution.

3. To promote and spread the practices of the values and principles proclaimed by the Constitution.

4. To defend, promote and contribute to the right to peace and encourage the culture of peace.

5. To work, in accordance to their physical and intellectual capabilities, in licit and socially useful activities.

6. To be formed in the educational system until graduation from high school.

7. To pay taxes in proportion to their economic capabilities, in accordance to law.

8. To report and fight against all of the acts of corruption.

9. To assist, feed and educate their sons and daughters.

10. To assist, protect and aid their ancestors.

11. To provide aid with all the necessary support, in cases of natural disasters and other contingencies.

12. To render mandatory military service, in case of males.

13. To defend the unity, sovereignty and territorial integrity of Bolivia, and to respect its symbols and values.

14. To guard, defend and protect the natural, economic and cultural patrimony of Bolivia.

15. To protect and defend the natural resources and contribute to their sustainable use, to preserve the rights of future generations.

16. To protect and defend an adequate environment for the development of living beings.

TITLE IV

JURISDICTIONAL GUARANTEES AND DEFENSE ACTIONS

CHAPTER ONE

JURISDICTIONAL GUARANTEES

Article 109.

I. All of the rights recognized in the Constitution are directly applicable and enjoy equal guarantees for their protection.

II. The rights and their guarantees can only be regulated by law.

Article 110.

I. The people that transgress constitutional rights will be subjected to the jurisdiction and competence of Bolivian authorities.

II. The transgression of constitutional rights makes its intellectual and material authors liable.

III. The attacks towards personal security makes its immediate authors liable, without serving as an excuse having committed them due to a superior order.

Article 111. The crimes of genocide, against humanity, and of treason to the country are imprescribable.

Article 112. The crimes committed by public servants that attempt against the patrimony of the State and cause grave economic damage, are imprescribable and do not admit the immunity regime.

Article 113.

I. The transgression of rights grants the victims the right to receive indemnity, reparation and compensation of damages and losses in a timely manner.

II.   In case the State is convicted to the patrimonial reparation of damages and losses, it shall file the action of repetition against the authority or public servant responsible for the action or omission that caused the damage.

Article 114.

I.   Any form of torture, disappearance, confinement, coercion, imposition or any kind of physical or moral violence is prohibited. The male and female public servants or public authorities that apply, instigate or consent to these, will be dismissed, without prejudice of the sanctions determined by law.

II.   The statements, actions or omissions obtained or undertaken through the use of torture, coercion, imposition, or by any other form of violence, are null to the full extent of the law.

Article 115.

I.   All persons will be timely and effectively protected by the judges and courts in the exercise of their rights and legitimate interests.

II.   The State guarantees the right to due process, to defense and to a justice that is plural, prompt, appropriate, gratuitous, transparent and without delays.

Article 116.

I.   Presumption of innocence is guaranteed. During the process, in case of doubt regarding the application of a norm, the most favorable to the accused or processed shall govern.

II.   Any sanction must be based on a law existing prior to the commission of the punishable act.

Article 117.

I.   No person can be convicted without having been previously heard and judged in accordance to due process. No one shall be subjected to criminal sanction that has not been imposed by a competent judicial authority as an executed judgment.

II.   No one shall be processed or convicted more than once for the same act. The reinstatement of the restricted rights will be immediate upon fulfillment of the sentence.

III.   No sanction consisting of deprivation of liberty may be imposed for debts or patrimonial obligations, except in the cases established by law.

Article 118.

I.   Infamy, civil death and confinement are prohibited.

II.   The maximum criminal sentence shall consist of thirty years of deprivation of liberty, without the right to pardon.

III.   The fulfillment of sanctions of deprivation of liberty and of security measures is aimed towards the education, rehabilitation and social reinsertion of the convicted individuals, with respect for their rights.

Article 119.
I.   During legal proceedings, the parties in conflict enjoy equal opportunities to exercise the faculties and rights that may serve in their benefit, whether in an ordinary process or in an indigenous originary farmer one.

II.   All persons have the inviolable right to defense. The State will provide a male or female defense attorney at no cost for the individuals accused or denounced, in the cases where these do not have the necessary economic resources.

Article 120.
I.   All persons have the right to be heard by a competent, independent and impartial jurisdictional authority, and cannot be judged by special commissions or subjected to other jurisdictional authorities other than those established prior to the case.

II.   All persons subjected to a legal proceeding must be judged in their language; exceptionally, in a mandatory manner, they shall be assisted by a male or female translator or interpreter.

Article 121.
I.   Within criminal matters, no person can be forced to declare against itself, or against its blood relatives up to the fourth degree or against its non-blood relatives up to the second degree. The right to remain silent will not be considered an indication of guilt.

II.   The victim within a criminal proceeding can intervene in accordance to law, and will have the right to be heard before each judicial decision. In case of not having the necessary economic resources, a male or female attorney will provide assistance free of charge.

Article 122. The acts of persons who usurp functions not competent to them, as well as the acts of those who exercise jurisdiction or authority not emanated from them, are null and void.

Article 123. The law only stipulates with regards to the future and will not have a retroactive effect, except in labor matters, when expressly determined in favor of the male and female workers; in criminal matters, when it benefits the accused male or female; in corruption matters, to investigate, process and sanction the crimes committed by public servants against the interests of the State; and in the other cases specified by the Constitution.

Article 124.

I.   Commits the crime of treason to the country the Bolivian male or female that incurs in the following acts:

    1.   For taking arms against its country, for joining the service of foreign participant states, or for entering into complicity with the enemy, in case of international war against Bolivia.

    2.   For violating the constitutional regime of natural resources.

    3.   For attempting against the unity of the country.

II.   This crime shall deserve the maximum criminal sanction.

CHAPTER TWO

ACTIONS OF DEFENSE

SECTION I

ACTION OF LIBERTY

Article 125. Anyone who considers its life in danger, who is illegally persecuted, or is unduly processed or deprived of personal liberty, can file a claim of Action of Liberty and appear, in an oral or written manner, on its own behalf or by anyone in its representation and without any procedural formality, before any judge or competent court in criminal matters, requesting the protection of his or her life, the halting of the unjustified persecution, and the reestablishment of the legal formalities or the restitution of his or her right to liberty.

Article 126.

I.   The judicial authority shall immediately set a day and hour for a public hearing, which shall take place within 24 hours from the filing of the claim, which shall state that the claimant be brought to its presence or shall attend the place of detention. With such order the citation will be executed, in person or through service of process, to the authority or person accused, an order that will be obeyed without observation or excuse, by the authority or the person accused as well as by the responsible of the jails or detention centers, without them, once served, being able to disobey.

II.   In no case can the audience be suspended. In the event that the defendant is absent, due to non-attendance or abandonment, it will be conducted in default.

III.   Knowing the background and having heard the allegations, the judicial authority, mandatorily and under responsibility, shall dictate sentence in the same audience. The sentence shall order the safeguarding of life, the restitution of the right to liberty, the reparation of legal defects, the cessation of the undue persecution or the remission of the case to a competent judge. In all cases, the parties will be notified with the lecture of the sentence.

IV.   The judicial ruling will be executed immediately. Without prejudice to it, the decision will be elevated for review, sua sponte, before the Plurinational Constitutional Court, within a term of twenty-four hours following its issuance.

Article 127.

I.   The public servants or individuals, who resist judicial rulings in the cases provided for this action, will be sent to the Public Ministry by order of the authority that had knowledge of the case to be criminally processed for attempting against constitutional guarantees.

II.   The judicial authority that does not proceed in accordance with what is set forth in this article shall be subjected to a sanction, in accordance to the Constitution and the law.

SECTION II

ACTION OF CONSTITUTIONAL PROTECTION

Article 128.   The Action of Constitutional Protection will take place against illegal or undue acts or omissions by public servants, or by individuals or collective persons, who restrict, suppress, or threaten to restrict or suppress the rights recognized by the Constitution and the law.

Article 129.

I.   The Action of Constitutional Protection shall be filed by the person who believes having been affected, by another with sufficient power of representation, or by the corresponding authority in accordance with the Constitution, before any competent judge or court, provided that there is no other mean or legal recourse for the immediate protection of the restricted, suppressed or threatened rights and guarantees.

II.   The Action of Constitutional Protection can be filed within a maximum term of six months, counted from the commission of the alleged violation or from the notification with the last administrative or judicial decision.

III.   The defendant authority or person will be summoned in the manner set forth for the Action of Liberty, with the objective of providing information and presenting, in its case, the facts regarding the denounced case, within a maximum term of forty-eight hours since the filing of the Action.

IV.   The final ruling will be pronounced in a public audience immediately following the reception of the information from the defendant authority or person and, in absence thereof, it will be made on the basis of the proof offered by the claimant. The judicial authority will examine the competency of the male or female public servant or the defendant person and, in case of finding the claim certain or effective, will grant the requested protection. The pronounced decision shall be elevated, sua sponte, for review before the Plurinational Constitutional Court within a term of twenty-four hours following the issuance of the ruling.

V.   The final ruling that grants the Action of Constitutional Protection will be executed immediately and without observation. In case of resistance, the case shall proceed pursuant to what is set forth in the Action for Liberty. The judicial authority that does not proceed in accordance with what is set forth in this article will be subjected to the sanctions established by law.

SECTION III

ACTION OF PROTECTION OF PRIVACY

Article 130.

I.   Any individual or collective person that believes to be unjustly or illegally impeded from knowing, objecting to, or achieving the elimination or rectification of the data registered in any physical, electronic, magnetic or computerized medium, in public or private files or data banks, or that affect its fundamental right to intimacy or personal or family privacy, or its own image, honor and reputation, can file the Action of Protection of Privacy.

II.   The Action of Protection of Privacy shall not proceed to eliminate secrecy in matters related to the press.

Article 131.

I.   The Action of Protection of Privacy shall take place following the procedure set forth for the Action of Constitutional Protection.

II.   If the competent court or judge admits the action, it shall order the disclosure, elimination or rectification of the data of which registration was challenged.

III.   The decision will be elevated, sua sponte, for review before the Plurinational Constitutional Court within a term of twenty-four hours following the issuance of the ruling, without suspending its execution.

IV.   The final ruling granted by the Action of Protection of Privacy will be executed immediately and without observation. In case of resistance, the case shall proceed pursuant to what is set forth in the Action for Liberty. The judicial authority that does not proceed in accordance with what is set forth in this article will be subjected to the sanctions established by law.

SECTION IV

ACTION OF UNCONSTITUTIONALITY

Article 132. Any individual or collective person affected by a judicial norm that is contrary to the Constitution will have the right to present the Action of Unconstitutionality, in accordance to the procedures established by law.

Article 133. The sentence that declares the unconstitutionality of a law, decree or any other kind of non-judicial resolution, makes the challenged norm inapplicable and takes full effect with regards to everyone.

SECTION V

ACTION OF COMPLIANCE

Article 134.

I.   The Action of Compliance will proceed in cases of non-compliance with constitutional provisions or the law by public servants, with the objective of guaranteeing the execution of the omitted norm.

II.   The action will be filed by the affected individual or collective person, or by another with sufficient power of representation, before a competent judge or court, and shall be processed in the same manner as with the Action of Constitutional Protection.

III. The final ruling will be pronounced in a public audience immediately following the reception of the information from the defendant authority and, in absence thereof, it will be made on the basis of the proof offered by the claimant. The judicial authority will examine the background and, in case of finding the claim certain or effective, will admit the action and order the immediate compliance of the omitted duty.

IV.   The ruling will be elevated, sua sponte, for review before the Plurinational Constitutional Court within a term of twenty-four hours following the issuance of the ruling, without suspending its execution.

V.   The final ruling granted in the Action of Compliance will be executed immediately and without observation. In case of resistance, the case shall proceed pursuant to what is set forth in the Action for Liberty. The judicial authority that does not proceed in accordance with what is set forth in this article will be subjected to the sanctions established by law.

SECTION VI

POPULAR ACTION

Article 135. The Popular Action proceeds against any act or omission by authorities or by individual or collective persons that violate or threaten to violate rights and collective interests, related to patrimony, space, security, public health, the environment and others of similar nature recognized by this Constitution.

Article 136.

I.   The Popular Action shall be filed during the period in which the violation or threat to the rights and collective interests continues. In order to file this action it is not necessary to exhaust the judicial or administrative processes already existent.

II.   This action can be filed by any person, individually or representing a collectivity and, in a mandatory manner, by the Public Ministry or Public Defender, when finding out about these acts while exercising their functions. The procedure for the Action of Constitutional Protection shall be applied.

CHAPTER THREE

STATES OF EXCEPTION

Article 137. In case of danger to the security of the State, external threat, internal commotion or natural disaster, the male or female President of the State will have the power to declare a state of exception, in all or in part of the territory were deemed necessary. The declaration of state of exception cannot in any case suspend the guarantees of the rights, the fundamental rights, the right to due process, the right to information and the rights of the persons deprived of liberty.

Article 138.
I.   The validity of the declaration of state of exception will depend on the subsequent approval of the Plurinational Legislative Assembly, which shall take place as soon as circumstances permit, and in all cases, within seventy-two hours following the declaration of the state of exception. The approval of the declaration will indicate the faculties granted and will keep strict relation and proportion to the case of necessity addressed by the state of exception. The general rights consecrated in the Constitution will not be suspended by the declaration of the state of exception.

II.   Once the state of exception has finished, no other state of exception can be declared within the following year, unless prior legislative authorization.

Article 139.
I.   The executive shall report to the Plurinational Legislative Assembly with regards to the reasons that gave place for the declaration of state of exception, as well as of the use made of the faculties conferred by the Constitution and the law.

II.   Those who violate the rights established in this Constitution shall be subjected to criminal prosecution for violation of rights.

III.   States of exception will be regulated by law.

Article 140.

I.   Neither the Plurinational Legislative Assembly, nor any other organ or institution, nor association or popular meeting of any type, can grant any organ or person any extraordinary faculty different to what is established in this Constitution.

II.   Public power cannot be accumulated, nor may any organ or person be granted supremacy over the rights and guarantees recognized in this Constitution.

III.   The reform of the Constitution cannot be initiated while there is a state of exception in force.

TITLE V

NATIONALITY AND CITIZENSHIP

CHAPTER I

NATIONALITY

Article 141.

I.   The Bolivian nationality is acquired by birth or by naturalization. Males and females are Bolivian by birth if they were born in the territory of Bolivia, with the exception of the sons and daughters of the foreign personnel of diplomatic missions; and if they were born abroad, from a Bolivian mother or Bolivian father.

Article 142.

I.   Foreign males and females in legal situation can acquire the Bolivian nationality if they have had three years of uninterrupted residence in the country under the supervision of the State, and they expressly manifest their will to obtain the Bolivian nationality and comply with the requirements established by law.

II.   The time of residence will be reduced to two years in case of foreign males and females who fit in one of the following situations:

    1.   Those that have Bolivian male or female spouses, Bolivian daughters or Bolivian sons, or Bolivian surrogate parents. Foreign male and female citizens who acquire the citizenship by marriage with a male or female Bolivian citizen do not lose it due to widowhood or divorce.

2.   Those that render military service in Bolivia at the required age and in accordance to law.

3.   Those that, because of their service to the country, are granted the Bolivian nationality by the Plurinational Legislative Assembly.

III.   The time of residence to obtain the nationality can be modified when there are reciprocal agreements with other states, mainly Latin-American.

Article 143.

I.   The Bolivian males and females who get married with foreign male and female citizens will not lose their nationality of origin. The Bolivian nationality will not be lost for acquiring a foreign citizenship.

II.   Foreign males and females who acquire the Bolivian nationality will not be obligated to renounce to their nationality of origin.

CHAPTER TWO

CITIZENSHIP

Article 144.

I.   All Bolivian males and females are citizens, and exercise their citizenship when turning 18 years of age, without regards to their levels of instruction, occupation or income.

II.   Citizenship consists in:

1.   In concurring as an elector or an eligible candidate in the formation and exercise of functions in the organs of the public power, and

2.   In the right to exercise public functions without any other requisite than suitability, except those established by law.

III.   Citizenship rights are suspended for the causes and in the manner set forth in article 28 of this Constitution.

SECOND PART

FUNCTIONAL STRUCTURE AND ORGANIZATION OF THE STATE

TITLE I

LEGISLATIVE ORGAN

CHAPTER ONE

COMPOSITION AND ATTRIBUTIONS OF THE PLURINATIONAL LEGISLATIVE ASSEMBLY

Article 145. The Plurinational Legislative Assembly is composed of two chambers, the Chamber of Deputies and the Chamber of Senators, and it is the only organ with faculties to approve and pass laws that govern within the entire territory of Bolivia.

Article 146.

I. The Chamber of Deputies is conformed of 130 members.

II. In each Department, half of the Deputies are elected in uninominal districts. The other half are elected by plurinominal departmental districts, from the lists headed by the candidates for President, Vice-President, and Senators of the Republic.

III. The Deputies are elected by universal, direct and secret suffrage. In the uninominal districts by simple majority of votes. In the plurinominal districts by means of the representation system established by law.

IV. The number of Deputies must reflect the proportional voting obtained by each party, citizen group or indigenous people.

V. The total distribution of seats between the departments will be determined by the Electoral Organ based in the number of inhabitants of each of them, in accordance to the last national Census, in accordance to Law. For equity, the law will assign a minimum number of seats to the departments with less population and less grade of economic development. If the distribution of seats for any department results uneven, there will be preference given to the uninominal seats.

VI. The uninominal electoral districts must have geographical continuity, affinity and territorial continuity, must not transcend the limits of each department and must base itself in population and territorial extension criteria. The Electoral Organ will limit the uninominal electoral districts.

VII. The special indigenous originary farmer electoral districts will be ruled by the principle of population density in each department. They must not transcend the departmental limits. They will only establish themselves in rural areas, and in those departments in which the indigenous originary farmer nations and people constitute a minority segment. The Electoral Organ will determine the special electoral districts. These electoral districts form part of the total number of deputies.

Article 147.
I. In the election of assembly members the equal participation of men and women will be guaranteed.

II. In the election of assembly members the proportional participation of the indigenous originary farmer nations and people will be guaranteed.

III. The law will determine the special indigenous originary farmer electoral districts, where neither the population density, nor the geographic continuity can be considered as conditional criteria.

Article 148.
I. The Chamber of Senators will be conformed of a total of 36 members.

II. In each department 4 Senators are elected in departmental districts, by universal, direct and secret suffrage.

III. The assignation of seats for the Senators in each department will be conducted through the proportional system, in accordance to law.

Article 149. To be a male or female candidate for the Plurinational Legislative Assembly, one must comply with the general conditions for access to public service, have eighteen years of age at the moment of the election, and have resided in a permanent manner for at least two years immediately prior to the election in the corresponding district.

Article 150.
I. The Plurinational Legislative Assembly will have alternate assembly members that will not receive remunerations except in the cases where they effectively served as alternates. The law will determine the manner of substitution of its members.

II. The assembly members shall not exercise another public function, under penalty of losing their mandate, with the exception of university teaching.

III. The resignation of an assembly member will be final, without having the possibility of requesting licenses or temporary substitutions with the purpose of exercising other functions.

Article 151.
I. The female and male assembly members will enjoy personal inviolability during the time of their mandate and afterwards, for the opinions, communications, representations, requests, parliamentary questions, accusations, proposals, expressions or any act of legislation, information or control, formulated or conducted while exercising their functions they cannot be criminally processed.

II. The address, residence or room of the male and female assembly members will be inviolable, and cannot be raided in any circumstance. This provision will be applied to the vehicles of their personal or official use and to their legislative offices.

Article 152. The male and female assembly members do not enjoy immunity. During their mandate, in criminal proceedings, the precautionary measure of preventive arrest will not be applied to them, except in crimes discovered in flagrance.

Article 153.
I. The male or female Vice-President of the State will preside the Plurinational Legislative Assembly.

II. The ordinary sessions of the Plurinational Legislative Assembly will be inaugurated on August 6th of each year.

III. The ordinary sessions of the Plurinational Legislative Assembly will be permanent and have two recesses of fifteen days each, per year.

IV. The Plurinational Legislative Assembly can hold sessions in different places other than the usual within the territory of the State, by decision of the Plenary and by notice of its female or male President.

Article 154. During recesses, the Assembly Commission will function, in the manner and with the attributions determined by the Rules of the Chamber of Deputies. In an extraordinary manner, for urgency issues, the Assembly can be called to meet by its male or female President, or by the male or female President of the State. It shall only consider the matters set forth in the convocation.

Article 155. The Plurinational Legislative Assembly will inaugurate its sessions on August 6th in the Capital of Bolivia, unless express notice by its male or female President.

Article 156. The duration of the mandate of the male and female assembly members is of five years, being able to be reelected for a single additional continuous term.

Article 157. The mandate of an assembly member is lost due to death, resignation, revocation of mandate, an executed convicting sentence in criminal cases or by unjustified abandonment of its functions for more than six continuous work days and eleven discontinuous throughout the year, as determined in accordance with the Rules.

Article 158.

I.   The attributions of the Plurinational Legislative Assembly, besides the ones determined by this Constitution and the law, are the following:

1.   To autonomously approve and execute its budget; appoint and dismiss administrative personnel, and attend to everything related to its economy and internal governance.

2.   To set the remuneration of the male and female assembly members, which, in no case, can be greater than that of the male or female Vice-President of the State. Receiving additional income from any other remunerated activity is prohibited.

3.   To dictate, interpret, derogate, abrogate and modify laws.

4.   To elect six of the members of the Plurinational Electoral Organ, by two-thirds vote of its members present.

5.   To pre-select the male and female candidates to conform the Plurinational Constitutional Court, the Supreme Court of Justice, the Agro-Environmental Court and the Judiciary Council.

6.   To approve the creation of new territorial units and establish their limits, in accordance to the Constitution and the law.

7.   To approve the economic and social development plan presented by the Executive Organ.

8.   To approve the laws in matters of budgeting, indebtedness, control and supervision of state resources of public credit and subsidies, for the undertaking of public works and social needs.

9.   To decide the indispensable economic measures of the country in cases of public necessity.

10. To approve the contracting of loans that compromise the general income of the State, and give the authorization to universities for the contracting of loans.

11. To approve the General Budget of the State presented by the Executive Organ. Once the bill is received, it shall be considered in the Plurinational Legislative Assembly within a term of sixty days. In case of not been approved during this term, the bill will be deemed approved.

12. To approve the contracts of public interest concerning natural resources and strategic areas, signed by the Executive Organ.

13. To approve the transfer of assets of public domain of the State.

14. To ratify international treaties subscribed by the Executive, in the manners established by this Constitution.

15. To establish the monetary system.

16. To establish the system of measures.

17. To control and supervise the Organs of the State and public institutions.

18. To question, at the initiative of any of the assembly members, the male and female Ministers of the State, individually or collectively, and agree on the censure by two-thirds vote of the members of the Assembly. The questioning can be promoted by any of the Chambers. The censure will imply the destitution of the male or female Minister.

19. To conduct investigations within the framework of its supervising attributions, through the commission or elected commissions for that purpose, without prejudice to the control conducted by the competent organs.

20. To control and supervise public companies, those of mixed capital and any entity where there is an economic participation by the State.

21. To authorize the use of military troops, armament and war material outside the territory of the State, and determine the reason and time for their absence.

22.   To exceptionally authorize the entrance and temporary transit of foreign military forces, determining the reason and time of permanence.

23.   At the initiative of the Executive Organ, to create or modify taxes of competence to the central level of the State. However, the Plurinational Legislative Assembly, at the request of one of its members, can request that the Executive Organ present bills regarding the matter. If the Executive Organ, does not present the requested bill within the term of twenty days, or the justification for not having done so, the representative who had requested it or another, can present his or her own bill for consideration and approval.

II.   The organization and functions of the Plurinational Legislative Assembly will be regulated by the Rules of the Chamber of Deputies.

Article 159. The attributions of the Chamber of Deputies, besides the ones determined by this Constitution and the law, are the following:

1.   To draft and approve its Rules.

2.   To qualify the credentials granted by the Plurinational Electoral Organ.

3.   To elect its executive committee and determine its internal organization and functioning.

4.   To apply sanctions to the male and female Deputies, in accordance to its Rules, by decision of two-thirds of the members present.

5.   To approve and execute its budget; to appoint and dismiss its administrative personnel and attend to everything related to its internal economy and internal regime.

6.   To initiate the approval of the General Budget of the State.

7.   To initiate the approval of the economic and social development plan presented by the Executive Organ.

8.   To initiate the approval or modification of laws regarding taxing, public credit or subsidies.

9.   To initiate the approval of the contracting of loans that compromise the general income of the State, and the authorization to universities for the contracting of loans.

10. To approve in each legislature the armed forces that need to be maintained during peace times.

11. To accuse, before the Chamber of Senators, the members of the Plurinational Constitutional Court, the Supreme Court and the Administrative Control of Justice for crimes committed during the exercise of their functions.

12. To propose lists of candidates to the male or female President of the State for the appointment of the male or female presidents of the economic and social entities, and for other positions in which the State participates in, by absolute majority in accordance to the Constitution.

13. To pre-select the candidates for the Administrative Control of Justice and send the names of the pre-qualified individuals to the Plurinational Electoral Organ so that it can proceed to the sole and exclusive organization of the electoral process.

Article 160. The attributions of the Chamber of Senators, besides the ones determined by this Constitution and the law, are the following:

1. To draft and approve its Rules.

2. To qualify the credentials granted by the Plurinational Electoral Organ.

3. To elect its executive committee and determine its internal organization and functioning.

4. To apply sanctions to the male and female Senators, in accordance to its Rules, by decision of two-thirds of the members present.

5. To approve and execute its budget; to appoint and dismiss its administrative personnel and attend to everything related to its internal economy and internal regime.

6. To be the sole instance to judge the members of the Plurinational Constitutional Court, the Supreme Court, the Agro-Environmental Court and the Central Administration of Justice for crimes committed while in exercise of their functions, with sentences approved by at least two thirds of the members present, in accordance to law.

7. To recognize with public honors those who are deserving for eminent services to the State.

8.   To ratify the promotions, proposed by the Executive Organ, for General of the Army, Air Force, Division and Brigade; for Admiral, Vice-Admiral, Rear-Admiral, and General of the Bolivian Police.

9.   To approve or deny the appointments of ambassadors and plenipotentiary Ministers proposed by the President of the State.

Article 161.   The Chambers will meet in Plurinational Legislative Assembly to conduct the following functions, besides those established in the Constitution:

1.   To inaugurate and close its sessions.

2.   To receive the oath of the male or female President and male and female Vice-President of the State.

3.   To accept or reject the resignation of the male or female President of the State and of the male or female Vice-President of the State.

4.   To consider the laws vetoed by the Executive Organ.

5.   To consider bills that, approved in the Chamber of origin, were not approved in the reviewing Chamber.

6.   To approve states of exception.

7.   To authorize the judging of the male or female President or of the male or female Vice-President of the State.

8.   To appoint the General Prosecutor of the State and the Public Defender.

CHAPTER TWO

LEGISLATIVE PROCEDURE

Article 162.

I.   The following have the faculty of legislative initiative, for its mandatory treatment by the Plurinational Legislative Assembly:

1.   The male and female citizens.

2.   The male and female assembly members in each of their chambers.

3.   The Executive Organ.

4.   The Supreme Court, in case of initiatives related to administration of justice.

5.   The autonomous governments of the territorial entities.

II.   The laws and the rules of each Chamber will develop the procedures and requirements to exercise the faculty of legislative initiative.

Article 163. The legislative procedure will be conducted in the following manner:

1.   The bill presented by an assembly member of one of the Chambers, initiates the legislative procedure in that Chamber, which shall remit it to the corresponding commission or commissions for its treatment and initial approval.

2.   The bill presented by another initiative will be sent to the Chamber of Deputies, which will remit it to the commission or commissions.

3.   The legislative initiatives in matters of decentralization, autonomies and territorial regulations will be received by the Chamber of Senators.

4.   When a bill has been informed by the corresponding commission or commissions, it will be sent for consideration by the plenary of the Chamber, where it will be discussed and approved in full and in detail. Each approval will require the absolute majority of the members present.

5.   The bill approved by the Chamber of origin will be remitted to the reviewing Chamber for its discussion. If the reviewing Chamber gives its approval, it will be sent to the Executive Organ for its enactment.

6.   If the reviewing Chamber amends or modifies the bill, it will be considered approved if the Chamber of origin accepts the amendments or modifications by the absolute majority vote of its members present. In case of not accepting the changes, the two Chambers shall meet at the request of the Chamber of origin within the term of the following twenty days to debate the bill. The decision will be made by the Plenary of the Plurinational Legislative Assembly by the absolute majority of its members present.

7.   In case thirty days pass without a pronouncement from the reviewing Chamber regarding the bill, the project will be considered by the Plenary of the Plurinational Legislative Assembly.

8.   The bill, once approved, will be remitted to the Executive Organ for its enactment as a law.

9.   A bill that was rejected may be proposed again during the following Legislature.

10.   The law approved by the Plurinational Legislative Assembly and remitted to the Executive Organ, can be observed by the male or female President of the State within ten working days from the time of its reception. The observations of the Executive Organ will be directed to the Assembly. If the latter should be in recess, the male or female President of the State shall send his or her observations to the Assembly Commission.

11.   If the Plurinational Legislative Assembly considers the observations of the President to be founded, it will modify the law accordingly and will return it to Executive Organ for its enactment. In case of not considering the observations to be founded, the law shall be enacted by the male or female President of the Assembly. The decisions of the Assembly will be made by the absolute majority vote of the members present.

12.   The law which is not observed during the corresponding period of time will be enacted by the male or female President of the State. The laws not enacted by the Executive Organ during the period of time set forth in the above numerals shall be enacted by the male or female President of the Assembly.

Article 164.

I.   The enacted law will be immediately published in the Official Gazette.

II.   The law will be of mandatory compliance since the day of its publication, unless another date for its coming into effect is specified therein.

TITLE III

EXECUTIVE ORGAN

CHAPTER ONE

COMPOSITION AND ATTRIBUTIONS OF THE EXECUTIVE ORGAN

SECTION I

GENERAL DISPOSITION

Article 165.

I.   The Executive Organ is composed of the male or female President of the State, the male or female Vice-President of the State, and the male and female Ministers of the State.

II.   The determinations adopted by the Council of Ministers make them collectively responsible.

SECTION II

PRESIDENCY AND VICE-PRESIDENCY OF THE STATE

Article 166.

I.   The male or female President and the male or female Vice-President of the State will be elected by universal, mandatory, direct, free and secret suffrage. The candidates elected as President and Vice-President will be the ones who received fifty percent plus one of the valid votes cast, or the candidates who received a minimum of forty percent of the valid votes cast, with a difference of at least ten percent in relation to the candidacy in second place.

II.   In case none of the candidacies meet these conditions, a second electoral round will take place between the two candidates who received the most votes, within a term of sixty days counted from the previous voting. The candidates who receive the majority of votes will be proclaimed President and Vice-President of the State.

Article 167.   To be a candidate for President or Vice-President of the State, one must satisfy the general conditions of access to public service, be thirty years of age on the day of the election, and have permanently resided in the country for a minimum of five years immediately prior to the election.

Article 168.   The mandate period of the male or female President and of the male or female Vice-President of the State is of five years, and they can be reelected only once in a continuous manner.

Article 169.

I.   In case of impediment or definitive absence of the male or female President, he or she will be replaced by the male or female Vice-President and, in the absence of the latter, by the male or female President of the Senate, and in his or her absence by the male or female President of the Chamber of Deputies. In this last case, new elections will be called within a maximum term of ninety days.

II.   In case of temporary absence, the Presidency of the State will be assumed by the Vice-President, for a period not greater than ninety days.

Article 170.   The mandate of the male or female President of the State will cease due to death; to resignation presented before the Plurinational Legislative Assembly; to a definitive absence or impediment; to an executive convicting sentence in criminal matters, to revocation of mandate.

Article 171.   In case of revocation of mandate, the male or female President of the State will immediately cease in his or her functions, with the Vice-President assuming the Presidency and immediately calling for elections for the Presidency of the State to take place within a maximum term of ninety days.

Article 172.   The attributions of the male or female President of the State, besides the ones determined by this Constitution and the law, are the following:

1.   To comply with and enforce the Constitution and the laws.

2.   To maintain and preserve the unity of the Bolivian State.

3.   To propose and direct the policies of the government and the State.

4.   To direct the public administration and coordinate the actions of the Ministers of the State.

5.   To direct foreign policy; subscribe international treaties; appoint public diplomatic and consular servants in accordance to law; and admit foreign officials in general.

6.   To request the calling for an extraordinary session of the Plurinational Legislative Assembly.

7.   To enact the laws approved by the Plurinational Legislative Assembly.

8.   To issue supreme decrees and resolutions.

9.   To administer the income of the State and decree its investment by means of the corresponding Ministry in accordance to the laws and with strict subjection to the General Budget of the State.

10.   To present the economic and social development plan to the Plurinational Legislative Assembly.

11.   To present to the Plurinational Legislative Assembly, during the first thirty sessions, the bill for the General Budget of the State for the following fiscal year and propose, during its term, the modifications considered necessary. The report regarding public expenses in accordance to the budget will be presented annually.

12.   To present annually to the Plurinational Legislative Assembly, in its first session, the written report regarding the course and state of the Public Administration during the yearly administration, accompanied by the ministerial reports.

13.   To enforce the judgments of the courts.

14.   To decree amnesty or pardon, with the approval of the Plurinational Legislative Assembly.

15.   To appoint, from among the lists of candidates proposed by the Plurinational Legislative Assembly, the male or female General Controller of the State, the male or female President of the Central Bank of Bolivia, the maximum authority of the Banks and Financial Entities Regulation Organ, and the male or female Presidents of the social and economic function entities with participation of the State.

16.   To preserve the security and defense of the State.

17. To appoint and dismiss the Commander in Chief of the Armed Forces and the Commanders of the Army, the Air Force and the Navy.

18. To appoint and dismiss the General Commander of the Bolivian Police.

19. To propose to the Plurinational Legislative Assembly the promotions to General of the Army, the Air Force, the Division and the Brigade; to Admiral, Vice-Admiral, and Rear-Admiral, and to General of the Police, in accordance to reports of their services and promotions.

20. To create and habilitate ports.

21. To appoint its representatives before the Electoral Organ.

22. To appoint the male or female Ministers of the State, respecting our plurinational character and gender equity within the composition of the ministerial cabinet.

23. To appoint the Attorney General of the State.

24. To present projects of bills of economic urgency, for consideration by the Plurinational Legislative Assembly, for priority treatment.

25. To hold the position of the male or female General Captain of the Armed Forces, and exercise this role for the defense, independence and territorial integrity of the State.

26. To declare a state of exception.

27. To exercise the maximum authority of the Agrarian Reform Service of Bolivia and to grant executable titles for the distribution and redistribution of land.

Article 173. The male or female President of the State may be absent from the Bolivian territory for official missions, without the authorization of the Plurinational Legislative Assembly, for a maximum period of up to ten days.

Article 174. The attributions of the male or female Vice-President of the State, besides the ones determined by this Constitution and the law, are the following:

1. To assume the Presidency of the State in the cases established the Constitution herein.

2.   To coordinate the relations between the Executive Organ, the Plurinational Legislative Assembly and the autonomous governments.

3.   To participate in the sessions of the Council of Ministers.

4.   To contribute with the male or female President of the State to the direction of the general policy of the Government.

5.   To participate jointly with the male or female President of the State in the formulation of foreign policy, as well as involvement in diplomatic missions.

SECTION III

MINISTRIES OF STATE

Article 175.
I.   The male or female Ministers of State are public servants and have the following attributions, besides those established in this Constitution and the law:

1.   To propose and contribute to the formulation of general policies of Government.

2.   To propose and direct the governmental policies of its sector.

3.   To manage the Public Administration of their corresponding branch.

4.   To dictate administrative norms within the area of its competence.

5.   To propose drafts of supreme decrees and subscribe them with the male or female President of the State.

6.   To resolve in last instance any administrative matter that corresponds to its Ministry.

7.   To present to the Plurinational Legislative Assembly any requested reports.

8.   To coordinate with the other Ministries the planning and execution of the policies of government.

II.   The male or female Ministers of State are responsible for the administrative acts adopted in their respective areas.

Article 176. To be appointed as a male or female Minister of State a person must satisfy the general conditions for entering public service; be twenty five years of age on the day of nomination; not be a member of the Plurinational Legislative Assembly; not be a director, shareholder or owner of a financial entity or company that has a contractual relationship or a conflict of interest with the State; not be the spouse, blood parent or be related to the second degree of whoever is acting as President or Vice President of the State.

Article 177. Cannot be appointed as a male or female Minister of State the person who, whether directly or as the lawful representative of a legal person, has the pending fulfillment of a contract or has executable debts with the State.

TITLE III

JUDICIAL ORGAN AND THE PLURINATIONAL CONSTITUTIONAL COURT

CHAPTER ONE

GENERAL DISPOSITIONS

Article 178.

I.   The power to impart justice emanates from the Bolivian people and is based on the principles of independence, impartiality, juridical security, publicity, probity, promptness, gratuity, legal pluralism, being interculturality, equity, service to society, citizen participation, social harmony and respect for rights.

II.   The guarantees of judicial independence are:

1.   The performance of the judges in accordance with the judicial career.

2.   The budgetary autonomy of the judicial organs.

Article 179.

I.   The judicial function is unique. The ordinary jurisdiction is exercised by the Supreme Court of Justice, the departmental courts of justice, the sentencing courts and the judges; the agro-environmental jurisdiction is exercised by the Agro-Environmental Court and its judges; and the indigenous originary farmer jurisdiction is exercised by their own authorities; there will be specialized jurisdictions regulated by the law.

II.   The ordinary jurisdiction and the indigenous originary farmer jurisdiction enjoy the same hierarchy.

III.   Constitutional justice is imparted by the Plurinational Constitutional Court.

IV.   The Judiciary Council is part of the Judicial Organ.

CHAPTER TWO

ORDINARY JURISDICTION

Article 180.

I.   The ordinary jurisdiction is based on the procedural principles of gratuity, publicity, transparency, orality, promptness, probity, honesty, legality, efficacy, efficiency, accessibility, immediacy, material truth, due process, and equality of the parties before the judge.

II.   The principle of refutation or impugnment within judicial processes is guaranteed.

III.   The ordinary jurisdiction will not recognize exemptions, privileges or extraordinary courts. The military jurisdiction will try the crimes of military nature regulated by the law.

SECTION I

SUPREME COURT OF JUSTICE

Article 181. The Supreme Court of Justice is the highest court of the ordinary jurisdiction. It is composed of male or female Magistrates. It is internally organized into specialized chambers. Its composition and organization will be determined by law.

Article 182.

I. The male or female Magistrates of the Supreme Court of Justice will be elected through universal suffrage.

II. The Plurinational Legislative Assembly will determine by two thirds of its members present the pre-selection of the male or female candidates for each department and will remit the names of those selected to the electoral organ so that it may solely and exclusively organize the electoral process.

III. The male or female candidates, or any other person, cannot conduct electoral campaigns in favor of the candidacies, under sanction of being disqualified. The Electoral Organ is the only responsible for spreading the merits of the male or female candidates.

IV. The male or female magistrates cannot belong to political organizations.

V. The male or female candidates who obtain a simple majority of the votes will be elected. The male or female President of the State will administer the oath of office.

VI. In order to become a Magistrate of the Supreme Court of Justice one must satisfy the general requisites established for public servants: be thirty years of age; have a law degree, having performed judicial functions, practiced as a lawyer or have been a university professor, honestly and ethically, for eight years and not have been sanctioned with dismissal by the Judiciary Council. The determination of merit will take into account the performance as an originary authority under its system of justice.

VII. The system of prohibitions and incompatibilities applied to the male or female Magistrates of the Supreme Court of Justice will be the same as the one applied to public servants.

Article 183.

I. The male or female Magistrates may not be re-elected. The period of their mandate will be of six years.

II. The male or female Magistrates of the Supreme Court of Justice will cease in their functions upon completion of their mandate, due to an executable sentence from a trial of responsibilities, resignation, death and the rest of the causes set forth in the law.

Article 184. The following are the attributions of the Supreme Court of Justice, besides those established by law:

1.   To act as a court of cassation and hear appeals of nullity in the cases expressly set forth by law.

2.   To resolve conflicts of competencies arising between the departmental courts of justice.

3.   To hear, resolve and request in one instance the extradition processes.

4.   To try, as a collegial court in plenary and in one instance, the male or female President of the State, or the male or female Vice-President of the State, for crimes committed while exercising their mandate. The trial will take place prior the authorization of the Plurinational Legislative Assembly, by decision of at least two thirds vote of its members present, and to a request supported by the male or female Prosecutor or General Prosecutor of the State who will formulate the accusation if believed that the investigation provides the basis for the conduction of the trial. The process will be oral, public, continuous and uninterrupted. The law will determine the procedure.

5.   To appoint, from the lists presented by the Judiciary Council, the voting members for the departmental courts of justice.

6.   To prepare projects of judicial laws and present them to the Plurinational Legislative Assembly.

7.   To know and resolve the cases of extraordinary revision of sentence.

Article 185. The magistrature of the Supreme Court of Justice will be exercised in an exclusive manner.

CHAPTER THREE

AGRO-ENVIRONMENTAL JURISDICTION

Article 186. The Agro-Environmental Court is the highest court specialized in the agro-environmental jurisdiction. It is governed specifically by the principles of social benefit, integrality, immediacy, sustainability and interculturality.

Article 187. To be elected the male or female Magistrate of the Agro-Environmental Court one must meet the same requirements as those for members of the Supreme Court of Justice, as well as having experience in the area and having performed well, ethically and honestly, in the agrarian judgeship, as an independent professional or as a university professor of the subject matter, for a period of eight years. During the pre-selection of the male or female candidates its pluralistic composition shall be guaranteed, considering criteria of plurinationality.

Article 188.

I.   The male or female Magistrates of the Agro-Environmental Court will be elected by universal suffrage, in accordance to the procedure, mechanisms and formalities for the members of the Supreme Court of Justice.

II. The system of prohibitions and incompatibilities applicable to the male or female Magistrates of the Agro-Environmental Court will be the same as for public servants.

III. The duration of the term, the permanence and cessation of the position established for the male or female Magistrates of the Supreme Court of Justice will be applied to the members of the Agro-Environmental Court.

Article 189. The following are the attributions of the Agro-Environmental Court, besides those established by law:

1. To resolve cassation and nullity appeals in actions regarding real agrarian, forestry, environmental, water, rights of use and enjoyment of natural renewable, freshwater, and forest resources, and biodiversity; complaints involving practices that endanger the flora, the fauna, the water and the environment; and complaints regarding practices that endanger the ecological system and the conservation of species or animals.

2. To know and resolve in sole instance the complaints of nullity and voidability of executable titles.

3. To know and resolve in sole instance the administrative contentious processes resulting from contracts, negotiations, authorizations, grants, distributions and redistributions of rights of use of natural renewable resources, and of the rest of the acts and administrative resolutions.

4. Organize the agro-environmental courts.

CHAPTER FOUR

INDIGENOUS ORIGINARY FARMER JURISDICTION

Article 190.

I. The indigenous originary farmer nations and people will exercise their jurisdictional functions and competency through their authorities, and will apply their own principles, cultural values, norms and own procedures.

II. The indigenous originary farmer jurisdiction respects the right to life, the right to defense and the rest of the rights and guarantees established in the Constitution herein.

Article 191.

I. The indigenous originary farmer jurisdiction is based on the specific link between the individuals who are members of the corresponding indigenous originary farmer nation or people.

II. The indigenous originary farmer jurisdiction is exercised in the following areas of personal, material and territorial effect:

1. The members of the indigenous originary farmer nation or people are subject to this jurisdiction, whether acting as plaintiffs or defendants, claimants or accusers, denounced or accused, or appellants or respondents.

2. This jurisdiction knows the indigenous originary farmer matters in accordance to what is established in the Law of Jurisdictional Demarcation.

3. This jurisdiction is applied to the relations and legal acts that are conducted or to the effects produced within the jurisdiction of the indigenous originary farmer nation or people.

Article 192.

I. Every public authority or person will obey the decisions of the indigenous originary farmer jurisdiction.

II. For the compliance of the decisions of the indigenous originary farmer jurisdiction, its authorities can request the support of the competent organs of the State.

III.   The State will promote and strengthen the indigenous originary farmer justice. The Law of Jurisdictional Demarcation will determine the mechanisms of coordination and cooperation between the indigenous originary farmer jurisdiction with the ordinary jurisdiction and the agro-environmental jurisdiction and with all of the constitutionally recognized jurisdictions.

CHAPTER FIVE

JUDICIARY COUNCIL

Article 193.
I.   The Judiciary Council is the instance responsible of the disciplinary regime of the ordinary, agro-environmental and specialized jurisdictions; the control and supervision of their administrative and financial management; and the formulation of administration policies. The Judiciary Council will be governed by the principle of citizen participation.

II.   Its conformation, structure and functions will be determined by law.

Article 194.
I.   The members of the Judiciary Council will be elected by universal suffrage from among the male or female candidates proposed by the Plurinational Legislative Assembly. The organization and implementation of the electoral process will be the responsibility of the Plurinational Electoral Organ.

II.   The members of the Judiciary Council of Justice will require, besides the general conditions of access to public service, to be thirty years of age, possess knowledge in the area of their attributions and having performed their duties ethically and honestly.

III.   The members of the Judiciary Council of Justice will remain in their positions for six years and cannot be re-elected.

Article 195. The following are the attributions of the Judiciary Council of Justice, besides those established by the Constitution and the law:

1.   To promote the revocation of the mandate of the male or female Magistrates of the Supreme Court of Justice and of the Agro-Environmental Court, when they, while in exercise of their functions, commit serious infractions as determined by law.

2. To exercise the disciplinary control over the male or female voting members, male or female judges; and auxiliary administrative personnel of the Judicial Organ. The exercise of this faculty will comprehend the possibility of cessation of their position for serious disciplinary infractions, expressly established by law.

3. To control and supervise the financial economic administration and all of the properties of the Judicial Organ.

4. To evaluate the performance of functions of the male and female administrators of justice.

5. To conduct legal and financial management audits.

6. To conduct technical and statistical studies.

7. To conduct the pre-selection of the male and female candidates for the formation of the departmental courts of justice who will be appointed by the Supreme Court of Justice.

8. To appoint, by means of a competitive process of evaluation of merit and examination of competency, the trial judges and instruction judges.

9. To appoint its administrative personnel.

CHAPTER SIX

PLURINATIONAL CONSTITUTIONAL COURT

Article 196.

I. The Plurinational Constitutional Court watches over the supremacy of the Constitution, exercises constitutional control, and safeguards the respect for and enforcement of constitutional rights and guarantees.

II. In its interpretative function, the Plurinational Constitutional Court will apply as a criterion for interpretation, with preference, the will of the constituent, in accordance to its documents, minutes and resolutions, as well as the literal content of the text.

Article 197.

I. The Plurinational Constitutional Court will consist of the male and female Magistrates elected on a basis of plurinationality, with representation from the ordinary system and the indigenous originary farmer system.

II.   The substitute male or female Magistrates of the Plurinational Constitutional Court will not receive remuneration, and will assume functions only in the case of absence of the titleholder, or for other reasons established by law.

III.   The composition, organization and functioning of the Plurinational Constitutional Court will be regulated by law.

Article 198.   The male or female Magistrates of the Plurinational Constitutional Court will be elected through universal suffrage, according to the procedure, mechanism and formalities of the members of the Supreme Court of Justice.

Article 199.

I.   To become a Magistrate of the Plurinational Constitutional Court, besides the general requirements to become a public servant, one must be thirty five years of age and have specialized or credited experience of at least eight years in the disciplines of Constitutional, Administrative or Human Rights Law. For the qualification of merits it will be taken into account having exercised as an originary authority under its system of justice.

II.   The male or female candidates for the Plurinational Constitutional Court will be proposed by organizations of civil society and of the indigenous originary farmer nations and people.

Article 200.   The term of service, permanence and cessation from their positions established for the male or female Magistrates of the Supreme Court of Justice will be applied to the members of the Plurinational Constitutional Court.

Article 201.   The male or female Magistrates of the Plurinational Constitutional Court will be governed by the same system of prohibitions and incompatibilities than for public servants.

Article 202.   The attributions of the Plurinational Constitutional Court are, besides those established by the Constitution and the law, to know and resolve:

1.   In sole instance, the matters of pure law regarding the unconstitutionality of the laws, the Autonomic Statutes, Organic Letters, decrees and all kind of non-judicial ordinances and resolutions. If the action has an abstract character, it can only be presented by the male or female President of the Republic, the Senators, Deputies, legislators, and maximum executive authorities of the autonomous territorial entities.

2.   The conflicts of competency and attributions between the organs of the public power.

3.   The conflicts of competency between the plurinational government, the autonomous and decentralized territorial entities, and among them.

4.   The appeals against fees, taxes, tariffs, patents, rights or contributions created, modified or suppressed in violation of what is set forth in this Constitution.

5.   The appeals against the resolutions of the Legislative Organ, when their resolutions affect one or more rights, regardless of whoever is affected.

6.   The reviews of the actions of Liberty, Constitutional Protection, Protection of Privacy, Popular action and of Compliance. This review will not impede the immediate and mandatory application of the resolution that resolves the issue.

7.   The consultations of the male or female President of the Republic, the Plurinational Legislative Assembly, the Supreme Court of Justice or the Agro-Environmental Court regarding the constitutionality of proposed bills. The decision of the Constitutional Court is of mandatory compliance.

8.   The consultations of the indigenous originary farmer authorities regarding the application of their legal norms as applied in a specific case. The decision of the Constitutional Court is mandatory.

9.   The prior control of constitutionality for the ratification of international treaties.

10.   The constitutionality of the procedure of partial reform of the Constitution.

11.   The conflict of competency between the indigenous originary farmer jurisdiction and the ordinary and agro-environmental jurisdictions.

12.   The direct appeals of nullity.

Article 203.   The decisions and sentences of the Plurinational Constitutional Court are binding and of mandatory compliance, and no subsequent ordinary appeal against them is allowed.

Article 204. The law will determine the procedures that will govern the processes brought before the Plurinational Constitutional Court.

TITLE IV

ELECTORAL ORGAN

CHAPTER ONE

PLURINATIONAL ELECTORAL ORGAN

Article 205.

I.   The Plurinational Electoral Organ is composed of:

    1.   The Supreme Electoral Court

    2.   The Departmental Electoral Courts

    3.   The Electoral Courts

    4.   The Suffrage Table Jurors

    5.   The Electoral Notaries

II.   The jurisdiction, competencies and attributions of the Electoral Organ and its different levels are defined, in this Constitution and the law.

Article 206.

I.   The Supreme Electoral Court is the highest level of the Electoral Organ, its jurisdiction is national.

II.   The Supreme Electoral Court is composed of seven members, all who remain in their functions during six years without the possibility of re-election, and at least two of which will be of indigenous originary farmer origin.

III.   The Plurinational Legislative Assembly, by two thirds vote of its members present, will elect six of the members of the Plurinational Electoral Organ. The male or female President of the State will appoint one of its members.

IV.   The election of the members of the Plurinational Electoral Organ will require a prior public announcement, and the qualification of their capabilities and merits through a public selection process.

V.   The Departmental Legislative Assemblies or Departmental Councils will select by two thirds vote of its members present, a list for each of the voting members of the Departmental Electoral Courts. From these lists the Chamber of Deputies will elect the members of the Departmental Electoral Courts, by two thirds vote of its members present, guaranteeing that at least one of its members belongs to an indigenous originary farmer nation or people from the Department.

Article 207. To be appointed a Voting Member of the Supreme and Departmental Electoral Courts, one must satisfy the general requirements for access to public service, be thirty years of age at the time of the appointment and have an academic formation.

Article 208.
I.   The Supreme Electoral Court is responsible for organizing, managing and executing the electoral processes and issuing their results.

II.   The Court will guarantee that the suffrage is exercised effectively, in accordance with article 26 of this Constitution.

III.   It is the function of the Supreme Electoral Court to organize and administer the Civil Registry and the Electoral Roll.

CHAPTER TWO

POLITICAL REPRESENTATION

Article 209. The male or female candidates for elected public positions, with the exception of the eligible positions of the Judicial Organ and the Plurinational Constitutional Court will be proposed through the organizations of indigenous originary farmer nations and people, citizens groups and political parties, in equality of conditions and in accordance to law.

Article 210.
I.   The organization and functioning of the organizations of indigenous originary farmer nations and people, citizens groups and political parties has to be democratic.

II.   The internal election of the male or female leaders and candidates of the citizens groups and political parties will be regulated and supervised by the Plurinational Electoral Organ, which will guarantee equal participation among men and women.

III.   The organizations of indigenous originary farmer nations and people can elect their male or female candidates in accordance to their own norms of communitarian democracy.

Article 211.
I.   The indigenous originary farmer nations and people can elect their political representatives in the corresponding instances, in accordance with their own forms of election.

II.   The Electoral Organ will supervise that the election of male or female authorities, representatives and candidates of the indigenous originary farmer nations and people through their own norms and procedures, is conducted in strict compliance with the norms of those nations and peoples.

Article 212.   No male or female candidate can run simultaneously for more than one elective position, or for more than one electoral district at the same time.

TITLE V

FUNCTIONS OF CONTROL, DEFENSE OF SOCIETY AND DEFENSE OF THE STATE

CHAPTER ONE

FUNCTION OF CONTROL

SECTION I

GENERAL CONTROLLER OF THE STATE

Article 213.
I.   The General Controller of the State is the technical institution that exercises the administrative control function of the public entities and of those in which the State has a participation or economic interest. The Controller has the faculty to determine signs of administrative, executive,

civil and criminal responsibility; it has functional, financial, administrative and organizational autonomy.

II.   Its organization, function and attributions, which must be based in the principals of legality, transparency, efficacy, efficiency, economy, equity, opportunity and objectivity, will be determined by the law.

Article 214. The male or female General Controller of the State will be appointed by two thirds vote of the members present of the Plurinational Legislative Assembly. The election will require a public prior announcement, and the qualification of the professional capacity and merits through a public process.

Article 215. To be appointed as the male or female General Controller of the State, one must fulfill the general requisites for access to public service; be at least thirty years old at the time of appointment; having obtained a professional degree in an area related to the position and have practiced as a professional for a minimum of eight years; having shown personal and ethical integrity, determined by a public observance process.

Article 216. The male or female General Controller of the State will exercise its functions for a period of six years, without the possibility of a new appointment.

Article 217.
I.   The General Controller of the State will be responsible for the supervision and the subsequent external monitoring of the public entities and of those in which the State has a participation or economic interest. The supervision and control will also be carried out over the acquisition, management and disposition of the strategic assets and services that are of collective interest.

II.   The General Controller of the State will present each year a report regarding its function of supervision of the public sector to the Plurinational Legislative Assembly.

CHAPTER TWO

DEFENSE OF SOCIETY FUNCTION

SECTION I

PUBLIC DEFENDER

Article 218.

I. The Public Defender will oversee the enforcement, promotion, spreading, and compliance of human rights, both individual and collective, that are established in the Constitution, the laws and in international instruments. The function of the Public Defender shall extend to the administrative activity of the entire public sector and to the activity of private institutions that provide public services.

II. The Public Defender will also promote the defense of the rights of the indigenous originary farmer nations and people, of the urban and intercultural communities, and of male and female Bolivians who are abroad.

III. The Public Defender is an institution with operational, financial and administrative autonomy, in accordance with the law. Its functions will be governed by the principles of gratuity, accessibility, speed and solidarity. While exercising its functions it does not receive instructions from the organs of the State.

Article 219.

I. The Office of the Public Defender will be headed by the male or female Public Defender, who will exercise its functions for a period of six years, without the possibility of a new appointment.

II. The Public Defender will not be subjected to prosecution, detention, accusation or trial for acts carried out while exercising its attributions.

Article 220. The male or female Public Defender will be appointed by at least two thirds vote of the members present of the Plurinational Legislative Assembly. The appointment will require a public prior announcement, and the qualification of the professional capacity and merits through a public process, among people recognized for their trajectory of defending human rights.

Article 221. To be appointed the male of female Public Defender one must fulfill the general requisites for access to public service; be at least thirty years old at the time of appointment and have proven personal integrity and ethics, determined through a public observance process.

Article 222. The attributions of the Public Defender are, besides those established by the Constitution and the law:

1. To file actions of Unconstitutionality, of Liberty, of Constitutional Protection, of Protection of Privacy, Popular actions, actions for Compliance and the direct appeal of nullity, without the requirement of empowerment.

2.   To present bills and modifications of laws, decrees and non-judicial resolutions in the matters of its competence.

3.   To investigate, sua sponte or at the request of a party, the acts or omissions that imply violations of the rights, individual and collective, that are established in the Constitution, the laws and international instruments, and request that the Public Ministry initiate the corresponding legal actions.

4.   To request information from the authorities and public servants with regards to the investigations that the Public Defender is conducting, to which no objection may be posed.

5.   To formulate recommendations, reminders of legal duties, and suggestions for the immediate adoption of corrective measures to all the organs and institutions of the State, and to issue public censure for acts or behavior contrary to these formulations.

6.   To have free access to the center of detention and prisons, to which no objection may be posed.

7.   To exercise its functions without interruption of any kind, even in the case of a declaration of a state of exception.

8.   To attend the persons who request its services promptly and without discrimination.

9.   To draft the regulations needed for the exercise of its functions.

Article 223.   The authorities and public servants have the obligation of providing the Public Defender with the information it requests with regards with the exercise of its functions. In case its request is not dully attended, the Defender will file the corresponding actions against the authority, who will be processed and dismissed if the noncompliance is proven.

Article 224. Each year, the male or female Public Defender will report to the Plurinational Legislative Assembly and to Social Control concerning the situation of human rights in the country and regarding the management of its administration. The Public Defender may be called at any moment by the Plurinational Legislative Assembly or by Social Control to provide a report with respect to the exercise of its authority.

SECTION II

PUBLIC MINISTRY

Article 225.

I. The Public Ministry will defend the legality and general interest of society, and will exercise the public criminal action. The Public Ministry has functional, administrative and financial autonomy.

II. The Public Ministry will exercise its functions in accordance with the principles of legality, opportunity, objectivity, responsibility, autonomy, unity and hierarchy.

Article 226.

I. The Prosecutor or General Prosecutor of the State is the highest hierarchal authority of the Public Ministry and exercises the representation of the institution.

II. The Public Ministry will have departmental prosecutors, prosecutors for specific matters and other prosecutors established by law.

Article 227.

I. The Prosecutor or General Prosecutor of the State will be appointed by at least two thirds vote of the members present of the Plurinational Legislative Assembly. The appointment will require a public prior announcement, and the qualification of the professional capacity and merits, through a public process.

II. The Prosecutor or General Prosecutor of the State will need to satisfy the general requirements for public servants, as well as the specific established for the Magistrature of the Supreme Court of Justice.

Article 228. The Prosecutor or General Prosecutor of the State will exercise its functions for six years, without the possibility of a new appointment.

CHAPTER THREE

DEFENSE OF THE STATE FUNCTION

SECTION I

ATTORNEY GENERAL OF THE STATE

Article 229. The Attorney General of the State is the institution of public juridical representation which has the attribution of promoting, defending, and safeguarding the interests of the State. Its organization and structure will be determined by law.

Article 230.

I. The office of the Attorney General of the State is composed of the male or female Attorney General, who will direct it, and other public servants as determined by law.

II. The appointment of the male or female Attorney General of the State will correspond to the male or female President of the State. The appointed person must comply with the requirements demanded for the Magistrature of the Supreme Court of Justice.

III. The appointment can be objected by decision of at least two thirds of the members present of the Plurinational Legislative Assembly, within a term not greater than sixty calendar days from the appointment. The objection will have as its effect the cessation of the functions of the appointed person.

Article 231. The functions of the Attorney General of the State are, besides those established by the Constitution and the law:

1. To defend the interests of the State judicially and extra-judicially, assuming its legal representation and intervening as the government representative with full rights in all judicial and administrative actions, within the framework of the Constitution and the law.

2. To present ordinary appeals and actions in defense of the interests of the State.

3. To evaluate and oversee the conduction of legal proceedings by the legal units of the Public Administration within the processes that are brought before the jurisdictional or administrative authorities. In the case of negligent action, it should urge the initiation of the appropriate actions.

4. To request the male or female public servants and other individuals the information considered necessary for the purposes of exercising its authority. This information may not be denied for any reason or cause; the law shall establish the corresponding sanctions.

5. To request the maximum executive authority of public entities the trial of the male or female public servants who, for negligence or corruption, cause damage to the patrimony of the State.

6.   To attend the complaints and claims made by citizens and entities which make up the Social Control, in the cases in which the interests of the State are harmed.

7.   To request to the General Prosecutor of the State to undertake the judicial actions that correspond for crimes committed against public patrimony of which it has knowledge.

8.   To present bills on matters related to its competence.

CHAPTER FOUR

PUBLIC SERVANTS

Article 232. The Public Administration is governed by the principles of legitimacy, legality, publicity, social commitment and interest, ethics, transparency, equality, competence, efficiency, quality, friendliness, honesty, responsibility and results.

Article 233. Public Servants are the male or female persons who perform public functions. Public servants form part of the administrative personnel, except for those who are in elected positions, those who are designated, and those who exercise functions of free appointment.

Article 234. To perform public functions, one must satisfy the following requisites:

1.   Have the Bolivian nationality.

2.   Be of legal age

3.   Having completed military duty.

4.   Not been subjected to a list of charges, or having executed convicting sentences in criminal matters, pending completion.

        5.   Not be included in the cases of prohibitions and incompatibilities established in the Constitution.

        6.   Be registered in the voting roll.

        7.   Speak at least two official languages of the country.

Article 235. The obligations of male and female public servants are:

1. To comply with the Constitution and the laws.

2. To fulfill its responsibilities, in accordance with the principles of public function.

3. To provide a sworn declaration of assets and income, before, during and after performing in the position.

4. To provide reports regarding the economic, political, technical and administrative responsibilities conducted while in exercise of the public function.

5. To respect and protect the assets of the State, and abstain from using them for electoral purposes or any other purpose outside of the public function.

Article 236. The following are the prohibitions for the exercise of the public function:

I. To perform simultaneously more than one full-time remunerated public job.

II. To act when its interests conflict with those of the entity its serves, and to enter into contracts or conduct business with the Public Administration, directly, indirectly or on behalf of a third party.

III. To appoint to public administration persons with whom there is a blood relation in the fourth degree and second of affinity.

Article 237.
I. The following are the obligations for the exercise of the public function:

1. To take inventory and care of the documents belonging to the public administration, with the prohibition of removing or destroying them. The law will regulate the management of archives and the conditions under which public documents may be destroyed.

2. To maintain the confidentiality of the classified information, which may not be disclosed even after the cessation of functions. The procedure for characterizing classified information will be set forth in the law.

II. The law will determine the sanctions in case of violating these obligations.

Article 238. The persons who fall within the following grounds for ineligibility cannot hold elective public office:

1. Those who have been or are directors of enterprises or corporations that have contracts or agreements with the State, and who have not resigned for at least three months before the day of the election.

2. Those who have been directors of foreign transnational enterprises that have contracts or agreements with the State, and who have not resigned for at least five years before the day of the election.

3. Those who hold elected positions, or who hold positions by designation or free appointment, who have not resigned from them, at least three months prior to the date of the election, with the exception of the President or Vice-President of the Republic.

4. The members of the Armed Forces and the Bolivian Police in active service who have not resigned for at least three months prior to the date of the election.

5. The ministers of any religious cult who have not resigned for at least three months prior to the date of the election.

Article 239. The following are incompatible with the exercise of the public function:

1. The acquisition or leasing of public assets on behalf of the public servant or third persons.

2. The signing of administrative contracts or obtaining any other kind of personal benefit from the State.

3. Exercising professional service as employees, representatives, advisors, managers of entities, companies or enterprises that have a contractual relationship with the State.

Article 240.

I. Any person who exercises a public position can be revoked from its mandate, with the exception of the Judicial Organ, in accordance to law.

II. The revocation of a mandate may be requested when at least half the term of the mandate has been completed. The revocation of a mandate cannot take place during the last year of the term in office.

III.   The revocation referendum will proceed by citizen initiative, at the request of at least fifteen percent of the voters of the electoral roll of the district that elected the public servant.

IV.   The revocation of a mandate of public servants will be conducted in accordance to law.

V.   The revocation of a mandate will result in the immediate cessation of service from the position, providing its substitute in accordance to law.

VI.   The revocation will take place only once during the constitutional mandate of the elected person.

TITLE VI

PARTICIPATION AND SOCIAL CONTROL

Article 241.

I.   The sovereign people, through the organized civil society, will participate in the design of public policies.

II.   The organized civil society will exercise social control of public management at all levels of the State, and of the public enterprises and institutions, mixed and private that administer public resources.

III.   It will exercise social control of the quality of public services.

IV.   The Law will establish the general framework for the exercise of the social control.

V.   The civil society will organize itself to define the structure and composition of social participation and control.

VI.   The entities of the State will generate spaces of participation and social control on the part of society.

Article 242.   Participation and social control implies the following, besides those established in the Constitution and the law:

1.   To participate in the formulation of the policies of the State.

2. To support the Legislative Organ in the collective construction of the laws.

3. To develop social control at all levels of the government and of the autonomous, self-sufficient, decentralized and deconcentrated territorial entities.

4. To generate transparent management of information and use of resources in all of the places of public management. The information requested for public monitoring may not be denied and shall be delivered in a complete, truthful, adequate and timely manner.

5. To formulate reports that support the petition for revocation of mandate, in accordance with the procedure established in the Constitution and the Law.

6. To know and comment on the management reports of the organs and functions of the State.

7. To coordinate the planning and control with the organs and functions of the State.

8. To file complaints with the corresponding institutions for investigation and processing, in the cases considered appropriate.

9. To collaborate in the public observation procedures for the appointment of the corresponding positions.

10. To support the electoral organ publicize the nominations of candidates for the corresponding public positions.

TITLE VII

THE ARMED FORCES AND THE BOLIVIAN POLICE

FIRST CHAPTER

THE ARMED FORCES

Article 243. The Armed Forces of the State are organically constituted by the Commander in Chief, the Army, the Air Force and the Navy of Bolivia, the forces of which shall be defined by the Plurinational Legislative Assembly at the proposal of the Executive Organ.

Article 244. The fundamental mission of the Armed Forces is to defend and preserve the independence, security and stability of the State, the honor and sovereignty of the country; to assure the supremacy of the Constitution; guarantee the stability of the legitimately constituted Government; and to participate in the integral development of the country.

Article 245. The organization of the Armed Forces rests on its hierarchy and discipline. It is essentially obedient, is not a deliberative body and is subject to the laws and military regulations. As an institutional organ it does not conduct any political activity; individually, its members enjoy and exercise the rights of citizens under the conditions established by the law.

Article 246.

I. The Armed Forces are subordinate to the male or female President of the State and receive their orders administratively through the male or female Minister of Defense, and with respect to technical aspects, from the Commander in Chief.

II. In the event of war, the Commander in Chief of the Armed Forces will direct the operations.

Article 247.

I. No male or female foreigner may exercise command, nor be employed or occupy an administrative position in the Armed Forces without the prior authorization of the Captain General.

II. To occupy the positions of Commander in Chief of the Armed Forces, the Chief of Staff, the Commanders and Chiefs of Staff of the Army, the Air Force, and the Navy of Bolivia, and of the large units, it is required to be a Bolivian by birth and meet the requisites set forth by law. The same requisites are necessary for the Vice-Minister of the Ministry of Defense.

Article 248. The Supreme Council of Defense of the Plurinational State, of which composition, organization and faculties will be determined by law, will be presided over by the Captain General of the Armed Forces.

Article 249. Every Bolivian will be obligated to render military service, in accordance with the law.

Article 250. The promotions in the Armed Forces will be granted in accordance with the respective law.

CHAPTER TWO

THE BOLIVIAN POLICE

Article 251.

I. The Bolivian Police, as a public force, has the specific mission of defending society and conserving public order, and to assure compliance with the law in the entire territory of Bolivia. It shall carry out the police function in an integral, indivisible manner and under a single command, pursuant to the Organic Law of the Bolivian Police and the other laws of the State.

II. As an institution, it does not deliberate or participate in political party activities, but individually its members enjoy and exercise their rights as citizens, in accordance with the law.

Article 252. The Bolivian Police Force is subordinate to the male or female President of the State, through the male or female Minister of Government.

Article 253. To be appointed Commander General of the Bolivian Police, it is necessary to be a Bolivian by birth, a General of the institution, and to satisfy the requisites established by law.

Article 254. In the event of international war, the forces of the Bolivian Police will be subordinated to the Commander in Chief of the Armed Forces for the time that the conflict lasts.

TITLE VIII

INTERNATIONAL RELATIONS, BORDERS, INTEGRATION AND MARITIME RESTITUTION

CHAPTER ONE

INTERNATIONAL RELATIONS

Article 255.

I.   International relations and the negotiation, subscription and ratification of international treaties respond to the objectives of the State in function of the sovereignty and interests of the people.

II.   The negotiation, subscription and ratification of international relations will be guided by the principles of:

1.   Independence and equality among states, no intervention in internal matters and a peaceful resolution of conflicts.

2.   Rejection and condemnation of all forms of dictatorship, colonialism, neocolonialism and imperialism.

3.   Defense and promotion of human, economic, social, cultural and environmental rights, with repudiation of all forms of racism and discrimination.

4.   Respect for the rights of the indigenous originary farmer nations and people.

5.   Cooperation and solidarity among states and peoples.

6.   Preservation of patrimony, capacity of management and regulation from the State.

7.   Harmony with nature, defense of biodiversity, and prohibition of forms of private appropriation for the exclusive use and exploitation of plants, animals, microorganisms and any living matter.

8.   Food security and sovereignty for the entire population; the prohibition of importation, production and trade of genetically modified organisms and toxic elements that harm health and the environment.

9.   Access of the entire population to basic services for their wellbeing and development.

10.   Preservation of the population's right to have access to all medications, primarily the generic ones.

11.   Protection and preference for Bolivian production, and encouragement for value added exports.

Article 256.

I.	The international treaties and instruments in matters of human rights that have been subscribed, ratified or those that have been joined by the State, which declare more favorable rights than those contained in the Constitution, will have preferential application over those in this Constitution.

II.	The rights recognized in the Constitution will be interpreted in agreement with international human rights treaties when these foresee more favorable norms.

Article 257.
I.	Ratified international treaties form part of the internal legal order having the rank of law.

II.	The international treaties that involve any of the following matters will require prior approval by binding popular referendum:

1.	Questions regarding borders.

2.	Monetary integration.

3.	Structural economic integration.

4.	The granting of institutional competences to international or supra-national organisms, in the context of integration processes.

Article 258. The procedures for the celebration of international treaties will be regulated by the law.

Article 259.
I.	Any international treaty will require approval by popular referendum when it is requested by five percent of the citizens registered in the voting roll, or thirty five percent of the representatives of the Plurinational Legislative Assembly. These initiatives can be also used to request the Executive Organ to sign a treaty.

II.	The announcement of a calling for a referendum will suspend, according to the time periods established by law, the process of ratification of an international treaty until the results are available.

Article 260.
I.	The denouncement of the international treaties shall follow the procedures established in the same international treaty, the general norms of international Law, and the procedures established in the Constitution and the law for its ratification.

II. The denouncement of the ratified treaties must be approved by the Plurinational Legislative Assembly before being executed by the male or female President of the State.

III. The treaties approved by referendum must be submitted to a new referendum prior to their denouncement by the President of State.

CHAPTER TWO

BORDERS OF THE STATE

Article 261. The territorial integrity, the preservation and the development of the border zones constitute a duty of the State.

Article 262.

I. The fifty kilometers from the borderline constitute the zone of border security. No foreign person, individual or company, may acquire property in this space, directly or indirectly, nor possess any property right in the waters, soil or subsoil, except in the case of state necessity declared by express law approved by two thirds of the Plurinational Legislative Assembly. The property or the possession affected in case of non-compliance with this prohibition will pass to the benefit of the State, without any indemnity.

II. The zone of border security is subject to a special legal, economic, administrative and security regime, oriented to promote and prioritize its development and to guarantee the integrity of the State.

Article 263. The defense, security and control of the zones of border security are the fundamental duties of the Armed Forces. The Armed Forces will participate in the policies of integral and sustainable development of these zones, guaranteeing its physical presence therein.

Article 264.

I. The State will establish a permanent policy of harmonic, integral, sustainable and strategic development of the frontiers, with the goal of improving the living conditions of its population, and especially the indigenous originary farmer nations and people living on the border.

II. It is the duty of the State to execute preservation and control policies for the natural resources in the border areas.

III. The regulation of the border system will be established by law.

CHAPTER THREE

INTEGRATION

Article 265.

I.   The State will promote, over the principles of a just and equitable relation with recognition of asymmetries, the relations of social, political, cultural and economic integration with other states, nations and peoples of the world and, in particular, the promotion of Latin American integration.

II.   The state will strengthen the integration of its indigenous originary farmer nations and people with the indigenous people of the world.

Article 266. The male or female representatives of Bolivia before supra-state parliamentary bodies emerging from the integration processes will be elected by universal suffrage.

CHAPTER FOUR

MARITIME RESTITUTION

Article 267.

I.   The Bolivian State declares its unforfeitable and imprescribable right over the territory that gives it access to the Pacific Ocean and its maritime space.

II.   The effective solution to the maritime disagreement through pacific means and the plain exercise of the sovereignty over such territory are the permanent and unforfeitable objectives of the Bolivian State.

Article 268. The development of the interests related to the oceans, rivers, lakes and the merchant marine will be the priority of the State, and its administration and protection will be exercised by the Bolivian Navy, in accordance to law.

THIRD PART

TERRITORIAL STRUCTURE AND ORGANIZATION OF THE STATE

TITLE I

TERRITORIAL ORGANIZATION OF THE STATE

CHAPTER ONE

GENERAL DISPOSITIONS

Article 269.

I.   Bolivia is organized territorially into departments, provinces, municipalities and indigenous originary farmer territories.

II.   The creation, modification and demarcation of the territorial units will be made by the democratic will of their inhabitants, in accordance with the conditions established in the Constitution and the law.

III.   The regions will form part of the territorial organization, in the terms and conditions set forth by law.

Article 270.   The principles that govern the territorial organization and the decentralized and autonomous territorial entities are: unity, voluntariness, solidarity, equity, the common good, self-government, equality, complementariness, reciprocity, gender equity, subsidiarity, gradualness, coordination and institutional faithfulness, transparency, public participation and control, provision of economic resources and the pre-existence of the indigenous originary farmer nations and people, under the terms established in this Constitution.

Article 271.

I.   The Autonomies and Decentralization Framework Law will regulate the procedures for the drafting of the Autonomic Statutes and the Organic Charters, the transference and delegation of competence, the financial economic regime, and the coordination between the central level and the decentralized and autonomous territorial entities.

II.   The Autonomies and Decentralization Framework Law will be approved by two thirds vote of the members present of the Plurinational Legislative Assembly.

Article 272. Autonomy implies the direct election of the authorities by the male or female citizens, the administration of its economic resources, and the exercise of legislative, regulatory, fiscal and executive authority by the organs of the autonomous government in the area of its jurisdiction, competence and attributions.

Article 273. The law will regulate the formation of the communities among municipalities, regions and indigenous originary farmer territories for the purpose of achieving their objectives.

Article 274. In the decentralized departments the election of the prefects and departmental councils shall be conducted by universal suffrage. These departments may become autonomous departments by referendum.

Article 275. Each deliberative organ of the territorial entities will draft in a participative manner the proposed Statute or Organic Charter which must be approved by two thirds of the total of its members, and prior constitutional review, will enter into effect as the basic institutional norm of the territorial entity by means of referendum to approve it in its jurisdiction.

Article 276. The autonomous territorial entities will not be subordinated among them and will have equal constitutional rank.

CHAPTER TWO

DEPARTMENTAL AUTONOMY

Article 277. The autonomous departmental government is composed of a Departmental Assembly, with deliberative, fiscal, and legislative departmental authority in the area of its competence and by an executive organ.

Article 278.
I.   The Departmental Assembly will be composed of male and female departmental assembly members, elected by universal, direct, free, secret and mandatory vote; and by departmental assembly members elected by the Indigenous originary farmer nations and people, in accordance with their own norms and procedures.

II.   The Law will determine the general criteria for the election of departmental assembly members, taking into account population, territorial, cultural identity and linguistic representation when there are indigenous originary farmer minorities, and parity and alternation of gender. The Autonomic Statutes will define its application in accordance with the specific realities and conditions of its jurisdiction.

Article 279. The departmental executive organ is directed by the male or female Governor, as its highest executive authority.

CHAPTER THREE

REGIONAL AUTONOMY

Article 280.

I. The region, composed of various municipalities or provinces that have geographic continuity and without transcending departmental limits, that share culture, language, history, economy and ecosystems in each department, will constitute a space of planning and management.

Exceptionally a region can be formed by a single province, which by itself has the characteristics that define a region. In the suburbs that are larger than 500,000 inhabitants, metropolitan regions can be formed

II. The Autonomies and Decentralization Framework Law will establish the terms and procedures for the orderly and planned formation of the regions.

Provincial authorities cannot be elected in the areas where regions are formed.

III. The region may establish regional autonomy, at the initiative of the municipalities belonging to it, by way of referendum in its jurisdictions. Its competences must be conferred by two thirds of the total votes of the members of the departmental deliberative organ.

Article 281. The government of each autonomous region will be constituted by a Regional Assembly with deliberative, normative-administrative and supervisory authority within the areas of its competence, and an executive organ.

Article 282.

I. The male or female members of the Regional Assembly will be elected in each municipality together with the lists of candidates for the municipal councils, in accordance with population and territory criteria.

II.   The region will draft its Statute in a participatory manner, in accordance with the procedures established for autonomous regions.

CHAPTER FOUR

MUNICIPAL AUTONOMY

Article 283. The autonomous municipal government will be constituted by a Municipal Council with deliberative, supervisory and legislative municipal authority within the area of its competence; and an executive organ, presided over by the male or female Mayor.

Article 284.

I.   The Municipal Council will be composed of male or female council members elected by universal suffrage.

II.   The indigenous originary farmer nations and people in the municipalities, which do not constitute indigenous originary farmer autonomy, may elect their representatives to the Municipal Council directly following their own norms and procedures and in accordance with the Municipal Organic Charter.

III.   The law will determine the general criteria for the election and determine the number of municipal council members. The Municipal Organic Charter will define its application, according to the specific reality and conditions of its jurisdiction.

IV.   The Municipal Council may draft the proposed Organic Charter, which will be approved according to what is set forth in this Constitution.

CHAPTER FIVE

EXECUTIVE ORGANS OF THE AUTONOMOUS GOVERNMENTS

Article 285.

I.   To be a male or female candidate for an elective position in the autonomous governments' executive organs, one must satisfy the general conditions for access to public service, and:

    1.   Have resided permanently in the corresponding department, region or municipality for at least the two years immediately prior to the election.

    2.   In the case of the election of the male or female Mayor and the regional authority, being twenty one years of age.

    3.   In the case of the election of the male or female Prefect or male or female Governor, being twenty five years of age.

II.   The mandate period of the highest executive authorities of the autonomous governments is five years, and they can be re-elected once for a continuous mandate.

Article 286.

I.   The temporary substitution of the highest executive authority of an autonomous government will correspond to a member of the Council or Assembly in accordance to the Autonomic Statute or the Organic Charter as the case may be.

II.   In the event of the resignation or death, permanent disability or revocation of mandate of the highest executive authority of the autonomous government, a new election will be conducted, provided that half of the term of the mandate has not elapsed. In contrary, the male or female substitute will be an authority already elected as defined in accordance to the Autonomic Statute or the Organic Charter as the case may be.

CHAPTER SIX

LEGISLATIVE, DELIBERATIVE AND SUPERVISORY ORGANS, OF THE AUTONOMOUS GOVERNMENTS

Article 287.

I.   The male or female candidates for the councils and assemblies of the autonomous governments must satisfy the general conditions for access to public service, and:

    1.   Have resided permanently in the corresponding jurisdiction for at least two years immediately prior to the election.

2.   Be 18 years of age on the day of the election.

II.   The election of the Assemblies and Councils of the autonomous governments will be conducted in separate lists from the executives.

Article 288. The mandate period of the members of the Councils and Assemblies of the autonomous governments will be of five years, and they may be re-elected once for a continuous mandate.

CHAPTER SEVEN

INDIGENOUS ORIGINARY FARMER AUTONOMY

Article 289. The indigenous originary farmer autonomy consists in self-government as an exercise of free determination of the indigenous originary farmer nations and people, of which population share territory, culture, history, languages, and their own juridical, political, social and economic organization and institutions.

Article 290.
I.   The formation of the indigenous originary farmer autonomy is based on the ancestral territories, currently inhabited by those nations and people, expressed in consultation, in accordance with the Constitution and the law.

II.   The self-governance of the indigenous originary farmer autonomies is exercised according to their norms, institutions, authorities and procedures, in accordance with their authority and competences, in harmony with the Constitution and the law.

Article 291.
I.   The indigenous originary farmer autonomies are indigenous originary farmer territories, and the municipalities, and regions that adopt that character in accordance to what is established in the Constitution and the law.

II.   Two or more indigenous originary farmer peoples can form a single indigenous originary farmer autonomy.

Article 292. Each indigenous originary farmer autonomy will draft its Statute according to its own norms and procedures, in conformity with the Constitution and the law.

Article 293.

I.   The indigenous autonomy based on consolidated indigenous territories and those in process, once consolidated, shall be constituted by the expressed will of the population through consultation in conformity with their own norms and procedures as the sole necessary requirement.

II.   If the conformation of an indigenous originary farmer autonomy affects the limits of municipal districts, the indigenous originary farmer nations or peoples and the municipal government must agree on a new district demarcation. If it affects municipal limits, a process shall be conducted before the Plurinational Legislative Assembly for its approval, prior the compliance with the requirements and particular conditions set forth by law.

III.   The law will establish the minimum population requirements and other differentiated for the constitution of an indigenous originary farmer autonomy.

IV.   To constitute an indigenous originary farmer autonomy of which territories are found in one or more municipalities, the law will state the articulation, coordination and cooperation mechanisms for the exercise of its government.

Article 294.

I.   The decision to form an indigenous originary farmer autonomy will be adopted in accordance to the norms and procedures for consultation, pursuant to the requisites and conditions established in the Constitution and the law.

II.   The decision to convert a municipality into an indigenous originary farmer autonomy will be adopted by referendum, in accordance to the requisites and conditions established by law.

III.   In the municipalities where there are indigenous communities with their own organizational structures of articulation and that have geographic continuity, a new municipality can be formed, following the procedure for its approval before the Plurinational Legislative Assembly, upon prior compliance with the requisites and conditions set forth in the Constitution and the law.

Article 295.

I.   To form an indigenous originary farmer region that affects municipal limits there shall be a prior procedure conducted before the Plurinational Legislative Assembly fulfilling the particular requisites and conditions set forth in the Constitution and the law.

II.   The addition of municipalities, municipal districts and/or indigenous originary farmer autonomies to form an indigenous originary farmer region, will be decided by referendum and/or in accordance with their norms and procedures for consultation as the case may be, and in accordance to the requisites and conditions established by the Constitution and the Law.

Article 296.   The government of the indigenous originary farmer autonomies is exercised through their own norms and forms of organization, with the denomination that corresponds to each town, nation or community, as established in their statutes and subject to the Constitution and the Law.

CHAPTER EIGHT

DISTRIBUTION OF COMPETENCES

Article 297.
I.   The competences defined in this Constitution are:

1.   Prerogative, those that the legislation, regulation and execution of which cannot be transferred or delegated, and which are reserved for the central level of the State.

2.   Exclusive, those which a level of government has legislative, regulatory and executive authority over a determined subject, been able to transfer and delegate the two latter.

3.   Concurrent, those in which the legislation corresponds to the central level of the State and the other levels simultaneously exercise the regulatory and executive faculties.

4.   Shared, those subject to basic legislation of the Plurinational Legislative Assembly of which development corresponds to the autonomous territorial entities, according to its character and nature. The regulation and execution will correspond to the autonomous territorial entities.

II.   Any competence not included in this Constitution will be attributed to the central level of the State, which may transfer or delegate it by law.

Article 298.
I.   The following are the prerogative competences of the central level of the State:

1.   Financial system.

2.   Monetary policy, Central Bank, monetary system, and the policy of foreign exchange.

3.   System of weights and measurements, as well as the determination of the official time.

4.   Customs regime.

5.   Foreign trade.

6.   State Security, Defense, Armed Forces, and Bolivian Police.

7.   Weapons and explosives.

8.   Foreign policy.

9.   Nationality, citizenship, laws applicable to foreigners, the right to asylum and refuge.

10.   Control of the borders with regards to the security of the State.

11.   Immigration regulation and policies.

12.   Creation, control and administration of the strategic public enterprises of the central level of the State.

13.   Administration of the patrimony of the Plurinational State and of public entities of the central level of the State.

14.   Control of air space and transit, throughout the entire national territory. The construction, maintenance, and administration of the international airports and inter-departmental air traffic.

15.   The Civil Registry.

16.   The official census.

17.   The general policy over land and territory, and their entitlement.

18.   Hydrocarbons.

19.   Creation of national taxes, rates and special tax contributions of tax domain of the central level of the State.

20.   General policy of Biodiversity and Environment.

21. Substantive and procedural codification in civil, family, criminal, tax, labor, commercial, mining and electoral matters.

22. National economic and planning policy.

II. The following are the exclusive competences of the central level of the State:

1. The national electoral regime for the election of national and sub-national authorities, and for national consultations.

2. General communications and telecommunications systems.

3. Postal service.

4. Strategic natural resources, which include minerals, the electromagnetic spectrum, genetic and biogenetic resources and water sources.

5. General system of hydraulic resources and services.

6. General system of biodiversity and environment.

7. Forestry policy and the general system for soils, forestry and woods.

8. Policy of generation, production, control, transmission and distribution of energy in the interconnected system.

9. Planning, design, construction, conservation and administration of the highways of the Fundamental Network.

10. Construction, maintenance and administration of the railroad lines and railroads of the Fundamental Network.

11. Public works of important infrastructure of the central level of the State.

12. Elaboration and approval of plans and official cartographic maps; geodesy.

13. Elaboration and approval of official statistics.

14. The granting of legal status to social organizations that conduct activities in more than one Department.

15. The granting and registration of legal status to Non-Governmental Organizations, Foundations and non-profit civil entities that conduct activities in more than one Department.

16. Social Security system.

17. Policies of the educational and health systems.

18. System of Real State Property Rights in mandatory coordination with the municipal technical registry.

19. Protected areas under the responsibility of the central level of the State.

20. Fiscal reserves with respect to natural resources.

21. Livestock health and safety.

22. Control of agrarian administration and rural land registry.

23. Tax policy.

24. Administration of Justice.

25. Promotion of the culture and conservation of important cultural, historic, artistic, monumental, architectural, archeological, paleontological, scientific patrimony, tangible and intangible of interest of the central level of the State.

26. Expropriation of real estate for reasons of public utility and necessity, in accordance with the procedure established by law.

27. Centers of information and documentation, archives, libraries, museums, periodical libraries and others of importance of the central level of the State.

28. Public enterprises of the central level of the State.

29. Rural human settlements.

30. Policies for basic services.

31. Labor policies and regime.

32. Ground, air, river and other transportation when it reaches more than one department.

33. Policies of territorial planning and land registry regulations.

34. Internal and external public debt.

35. General policies of productive development.

36. General housing policies.

37. General tourism policies.

38. Land regime. The law will determine the faculties to be transferred or delegated to the autonomies.

Article 299.

I. The following competences are exercised in shared manner between the central level of the State and the autonomous territorial entities:
1. The departmental and municipal electoral systems.

2. Fixed and mobile telephone and telecommunications services.

3. Urban electrification.

4. Lottery games and gambling.

5. International relations within the framework of the foreign policy of the State.

6. The establishment of citizen Conciliation Instances for the resolution of conflicts between neighbors in municipal matters.

7. Regulation for the creation and/or modification of taxes that are of exclusive domain of the autonomous governments.

II. The following authorities will be exercised concurrently by the central level of the State and the autonomous territorial entities:

1. To preserve, conserve and contribute to the protection of the environment and the wild fauna maintaining the ecological equilibrium and controlling environmental pollution.

2. Management of the health and educational systems.

3. Science, technology and research.

4. Conservation of soils, forestry resources and forests.

5. Weather Service.

6.   Electromagnetic frequencies in the areas of their jurisdiction and within the framework of the policies of the State.

7.   Promotion and administration of hydraulic and energy projects.

8.   Industrial waste and toxic materials.

9.   Potable water projects and treatment of solid waste.

10.   Irrigation projects.

11.   Protection of basins.

12.   Administration or river ports.

13.   Public security.

14.   Government control system.

15.   Housing and social housing.

16.   Agriculture, livestock, hunting and fishing.

Article 300.
I.   The autonomous departmental governments have exclusive competence over the following in their jurisdictions:

1.   To elaborate their Statute pursuant to the procedures established in the Constitution and the Law.

2.   To plan and develop human development in their jurisdiction.

3.   To initiate and announce departmental consultations and referendums on matters within their competence.

4.   Promotion of employment and improvement of working conditions, within the framework of national policies.

5.   Elaboration and execution of the Plans of Territorial Zoning and use of soils, in coordination with the plans of the central level of the State municipalities and indigenous originary farmer.

6.   Projects of generation and transport of energy in isolated systems.

7.   Planning, design, construction, conservation and administration of the highways of the departmental network in accordance with state

policies, including those of the Fundamental Network in the absence of the central level, in accordance with the norms established thereby.

8. Construction and maintenance of rail lines and railroads in the department in accordance with state policies, in accordance to the norms established by the state.

9. Inter-province ground, river, railroad and other means of transportation in the department.

10. Construction, maintenance and administration of the public departmental airports.

11. Departmental statistics.

12. The granting of legal personality to public organizations that conduct activities in the department.

13. The granting of legal personality to Non-Governmental Organizations, foundations and non-profit civil entities that conduct activities in the department.

14. Agricultural health and safety services.

15. Projects for rural electrification.

16. Projects of alternative and renewable sources of energy within the department preserving food security.

17. Sports in the area of its jurisdiction.

18. Promotion and conservation of the departmental natural patrimony.

19. Promotion and conservation of culture, cultural, historic, artistic, monumental, architectural, archeological, paleontological, scientific, tangible and intangible departmental patrimony.

20. Departmental tourism policies.

21. Projects for departmental infrastructure to support production.

22. Creation and administration of taxes of departmental character, of which imposition will not be analogous to the national or municipal taxes.

23. Creation and administration of fees and special contributions of departmental character.

24. Commerce, industry and services for development and competitiveness within the department.

25. Expropriation of real estate in its jurisdiction for reasons of public departmental utility and necessity, in accordance to the procedure established by Law, as well as the establishment of administrative limitations and rights of way in properties, for reasons of technical and legal order and for public interest.

26. To elaborate, approve and execute is programs of operation and its budget.

27. Fiduciary funds, investment funds and mechanisms of transfer of resources necessary and inherent to its competences.

28. Departmental centers of information and documentation, archives, libraries, museums, periodical libraries and others.

29. Departmental public enterprises.

30. Promotion and development of projects and policies for children and adolescents, women, the elderly and persons with disabilities.

31. Promotion and administration of services for productive and agricultural development.

32. Elaboration and execution of departmental economic and social development plans.

33. To participate in industrialization, distribution and commercialization enterprises of hydrocarbons in the departmental territory in association with the national entities of the sector.

34. Promotion of private investment in the department within the framework of the national economic policies.

35. Planning of departmental development in concordance with national planning.

36. Administration of the royalties received within the framework of the general budget of the nation, which will be transferred automatically to the Departmental Treasury.

II.   The Departmental Autonomic Statues may define as concurrent some of the exclusive competences, with other territorial entities of the department.

III.   The competences that are transferred or delegated will also be of departmental execution.

Article 301. The region, once constituted as a regional autonomy, will receive the competences that may be transferred or delegated.

Article 302.
I.   The autonomous municipal governments have exclusive competence over the following in their jurisdictions:

1.   To draft the Municipal Organic Charter in accordance to the procedures established in this Constitution and the law.

2.   To plan and promote human development in their jurisdiction.

3.   To initiate and announce municipal consultations and referendums on matters within their competence.

4.   Promotion of employment and improvement of working conditions within the framework of national policies.

5.   To preserve, conserve and contribute to the protection of the environment and natural resources, wild fauna and domestic animals.

6.   Elaboration of the Plans of Territorial Zoning and use of soils, in coordination with the plans of the central level of the State, departmental and indigenous originary farmer.

7.   Planning, design, construction, conservation and administration of neighborhood roads in coordination with the indigenous originary farmer peoples when it corresponds.

8.   Construction, maintenance and administration of public local airports.

9.   Municipal statistics.

10.   The urban land registry in the area of their jurisdiction in conformity to the precepts and technical parameters established by the Municipal Governments.

11. Municipally protected areas in accordance with the parameters and conditions established by the Municipal Governments.

12. Projects of alternative and renewable sources of energy preserving food security of municipality reach.

13. To control the quality and sanitary elaboration, transport and sale of food products for human and animal consumption.

14. Sports in the area of their jurisdiction.

15. Promotion and conservation of the natural municipal patrimony.

16. Promotion and conservation of culture and municipal cultural, historic, artistic, monumental, architectural, archeological, paleontological, scientific, tangible and intangible municipal patrimony.

17. Local tourism policies.

18. Urban transportation, automobile ownership registry, road regulation and education, urban traffic administration and control.

19. Creation and administration of taxes of municipal character, of which imposition will not be analogous to the national or departmental taxes.

20. Creation and administration of fees, certificates for economic activity and special contributions of municipal character.

21. Projects for productive infrastructure.

22. Expropriation of real estate in its jurisdiction for reasons of public municipal utility and necessity, in accordance to the procedure established by Law, as well as the establishment of administrative limitations and rights of way in properties, for reasons of technical and legal order and for public interest.

23. To elaborate, approve and execute is programs of operation and its budget.

24. Fiduciary funds, investment funds and mechanisms of transfer of resources necessary and inherent to its competences.

25. Municipal centers of information and documentation, archives, libraries, museums, periodical libraries and others.

26.   Public municipal enterprises.

27.   Urban sanitation, management and treatment of solid waste within the framework of State policy.

28.   To design, construct, equip and maintain the infrastructure and works of public interest and the assets of municipal domain, within its jurisdictional territory.

29.   Urban development and urban settlements.

30.   Public lighting service in its jurisdiction.

31.   Promotion of cultural and artistic activities in its jurisdiction.

32.   Public shows and recreational games.

33.   Urban advertising and announcements.

34.   To promote and sign agreements of association or municipal community with other municipalities.

35.   Agreements and/or contracts with natural or collective persons, public and private, for the development and fulfillment of their attributions, competences and purposes.

36.   To constitute and regulate the Municipal Guard to contribute to the fulfillment, exercise and execution of its competences as well as the compliance with the municipal norms and the issued resolutions.

37.   Policies that guarantee the defense of consumers and users in the municipal area.

38.   Systems of micro-irrigation in coordination with the indigenous originary farmer people.

39.   Promotion and development of projects and policies for children and adolescents, women, the elderly and persons with disabilities.

40.   Basic services as well as the approval of the corresponding fees in its jurisdiction.

41.   Grains and sharecroppers, in coordination with the indigenous originary farmer people, when it corresponds.

42.   Planning of municipal development in concordance with the departmental and national planning.

43.   To participate in enterprises of industrialization, distribution and commercialization of Hydrocarbons in the municipal territory in association with the national entities of the sector.

II.   The competences that are transferred or delegated will also be of municipal execution.

Article 303.

I.   The indigenous originary farmer autonomy, in addition to its competences shall assume those of the municipalities, in accordance with a process of institutional development and with their own cultural characteristics in conformity with the Constitution and the Autonomies and Decentralization Framework Law.

II.   The indigenous originary farmer region, will assume the competences that may be transferred or delegated to it.

Article 304.

I.   The indigenous originary farmer autonomies can exercise the following exclusive competences:

1.   Elaborate their Statute for the exercise of their autonomy in accordance to the Constitution and the Law.

2.   Definition and management of their own forms of economic, social, political, organizational and cultural development, in accordance with their identity and the vision of each village.

3.   Management and administration of renewable natural resources, in accord with the Constitution.

4.   Elaboration of Plans of Territorial Zoning and use of soils, in coordination with the plans of the central level of the State, departmental and municipal.

5.   Electrification in isolated systems in their jurisdiction.

6.   Maintenance and administration of local and communal roads.

7.   Administration and preservation of protected areas in their jurisdiction, within the framework of the policy of the State.

8.   Exercise of the indigenous originary farmer jurisdiction for the application of justice and the resolution of conflicts through their

own norms and procedures in accordance with the Constitution and the law.

9.   Sports, leisure activities and recreation.

10.   Tangible and intangible cultural patrimony. The safeguard, encouragement and promotion of its cultures, art, identity, archeological centers, religious and cultural places, and museums.

11.   Tourism policies.

12.   To create and administer fees, certificates and special contributions in the area of its jurisdiction in accordance with the law.

13.   Administer the taxes within its competence in the area of its jurisdiction.

14.   To elaborate, approve and execute its programs of operation and its budget.

15.   Planning and management of territorial occupation.

16.   Housing, town planning and redistribution of population in accordance with the cultural practices in the area of its jurisdiction.

17.   To promote and subscribe agreements of cooperation with other towns and public and private entities.

18.   Maintenance and administration of its micro-irrigation systems.

19.   Encouragement and development of productive activity.

20.   Construction, maintenance and administration of the infrastructure necessary for development in its jurisdiction.

21.   Participate, develop and execute the mechanisms of prior, free and informed consultation related to the application of legislative, executive and administrative measures that affect them.

22.   Preservation of the habitat and the landscape, in accordance with its principles, norms, and cultural, technological, space and historical practices.

23.   Development and exercise of its democratic institutions in accordance to its own norms and procedures.

II. The indigenous originary farmer autonomies can exercise the following shared competences:

1. International exchanges within the framework of the foreign policy of the State.

2. Participation and control in the use of grains.

3. The safeguard and registration of collective intellectual property related to knowledge of genetic resources, traditional medicine and germ plasma, in accordance with the law.

4. Control and regulation of foreign institutions and organizations that conduct activities in their jurisdiction, which are inherent to the development of their institutions, culture, environment and natural patrimony.

III. The indigenous originary farmer autonomies may exercise the following concurrent competences:

1. Organization, planning and execution of the health policy in their jurisdiction.

2. Organization, planning and execution of plans, programs and projects related to education, science, technology and research, within the framework of State legislation.

3. Conservation of forestry resources, biodiversity and the environment.

4. Irrigation systems, water resources, sources of water and energy, within the framework of State policy, within their jurisdiction.

5. Construction of micro-irrigation systems.

6. Construction of local and communal roads.

7. Promotion for the construction of productive infrastructures.

8. Promotion and encouragement of agriculture and stockbreeding.

9. Control and socio-environmental monitoring of the hydrocarbon and mining activities conducted in their jurisdiction.

10. Systems of financial control and administration of assets and services.

IV.   The resources necessary for the fulfillment of their competences will be transferred automatically by the Plurinational State in accordance to law.

Article 305. Every assignment or transfer of competences must be accompanied by the determination of the source of economic and financial resources necessary for its exercise.

FOURTH PART

ECONOMIC STRUCTURE AND ORGANIZATION OF THE STATE

TITLE I

ECONOMIC ORGANIZATION OF THE STATE

CHAPTER ONE

GENERAL DISPOSITIONS

Article 306.

I.   The Bolivian economic model is plural and seeks to improve the quality of life and the living well of all Bolivians.

II.   The plural economy is constituted by forms of community, state, private and public cooperative economic organization.

III.   The plural economy articulates different forms of economic organization based on the principles of complementariness, reciprocity, solidarity, redistribution, equality, legal security, sustainability, equilibrium, justice and transparency.   The social and communitarian economy will complement the individual interest with the collective wellbeing.

IV.   The forms of economic organization recognized in this Constitution may form mixed companies.

V.   The State places the highest value on human beings and assures development through the equitable redistribution of the economic surplus in the social policies related to health, education, culture, and the re-investment in productive economic development.

Article 307. The State will recognize, respect, protect and promote communitarian economic development. This form of communitarian economic organization includes the systems of production and reproduction of public life, founded on the principles and visions of the indigenous originary farmer nations and people.

Article 308.

I. The State recognizes, respects and protects private initiative that contributes to the economic and social development and the strengthening of the economic independence of the country.

II. Free enterprise and full exercise of business activities, which shall be regulated by law, are guaranteed.

Article 309. The form of state economic organization includes the enterprises and other economic entities that are property of the State, which shall comply with the following objectives:

1. To administer property rights over natural resources on behalf of the Bolivian people, and to exercise strategic control of the productive chain and industrialization of these resources.

2. To manage basic services of potable water and sewer systems directly or by means of public, communitarian, cooperative or mixed enterprises.

3. To directly produce goods and services.

4. To promote economic democracy and achieve the food sovereignty of the population.

5. To guarantee social participation and control over its organization and management, as well as the participation of workers in decision making and in the profits.

Article 310. The State recognizes and protects cooperatives as forms of labor of solidarity and cooperation, which do not seek profit. The organization of cooperatives will be promoted mainly in production activities.

Article 311.

I. All forms of economic organization established in this Constitution will enjoy equality before the law.

II. The plural economy comprises the following aspects:

1. The State will exercise the integral direction of the economic development and their planning processes.

2.   The natural resources are the property of the Bolivian people and will be managed by the State. Individual and collective property land rights will be respected and guaranteed. Agriculture, stockbreeding, as well as hunting and fishing not involving protected species, are activities that are governed by what is established in Part Four of this Constitution relating to the economic structure and organization of the State.

3.   The industrialization of natural resources to overcome the dependence on the export of raw materials and to achieve an economy with a productive base, within the framework of sustainable development, in harmony with nature.

4.   The State may intervene in every part of the productive chain of the strategic sectors, seeking to guarantee its supply in order to preserve the quality of life of all male and female Bolivians.

5.   Respect for enterprise initiative and legal security.

6.   The State will encourage and promote the communitarian area of the economy as a supportive alternative in rural and urban areas.

Article 312.

I.   Every economic activity must contribute to the strengthening of the economic sovereignty of the country. The private accumulation of economic power to the degree that it might endanger the economic sovereignty of the State will not be permitted.

II.   All forms of economic organization have the obligation to generate dignified work and to contribute to the reduction of inequalities and to the eradication of poverty.

III.   All forms of economic organization have the obligation to protect the environment.

Article 313. To eliminate poverty and social and economic exclusion, and in order to achieve living well in its multiple dimensions, the economic organization of Bolivia has the following goals:

1.   The generation of social wealth within the framework of respect for individual rights, as well as the rights of the peoples and nations.

2.   The fair production, distribution and redistribution of wealth and economic surplus.

3.   The reduction of inequality of access to productive resources.

4.   The reduction of regional inequalities.

5.   The industrializing productive development of natural resources.

6.   The active participation of the public and communitarian economies in the productive apparatus.

Article 314. Private monopoly and oligopoly are prohibited, as well as any other form of association or agreement of private natural or legal persons, Bolivian or foreign, which attempt to control and have exclusivity over the production and commercialization of goods and services.

Article 315.

I.   The State recognizes the property of land of all legal persons that are legally constituted in the national territory provided that its use serves to fulfill the objective of the creation of an economic agent, the generation of employment, and the production and commercialization of goods and/or services.

II.   The legal persons mentioned in the paragraph above that are formed after the adoption of the Constitution herein will have a corporate structure with the number of owners no less than the division of the total surface by five thousand hectares, rounding up the result to the immediately higher whole number.

CHAPTER TWO

FUNCTION OF THE STATE IN THE ECONOMY

Article 316. The function of the State in the economy consists in:

1.   Conducting the process of economic and social planning, with the participation of, and in consultation with, the citizens. The law will establish a system of comprehensive state planning, which will incorporate all the territorial entities.

2.   Directing the economy and regulating the processes of production, distribution and commercialization of goods and services, according to the principles established in this Constitution.

3.   Exercising the direction and control of the strategic sectors of the economy.

4. Directly participating in the economy by way of incentives and the production of economic and social goods and services in order to promote economic and social equity, and to encourage development, preventing an oligopolistic control of the economy.

5. Promoting the integration of different economic forms of production, with the objective of achieving economic and social development.

6. Promoting primarily the industrialization of renewable and nonrenewable natural resources, within the framework of respect for and protection of the environment, in order to guarantee the generation of employment and the economic and social goods for the population.

7. Promoting policies of equitable distribution of wealth and of the economic resources of the country, for the purpose of preventing inequality, social and economic exclusion, and to eradicate poverty in its multiple dimensions.

8. Establishing state monopoly over productive and commercial activities that are considered indispensable in the event of pubic need.

9. Periodically formulating, with the participation of and in consultation with the citizens, the general development plan, the execution of which is mandatory for every form of economic organization.

10. To administer economic resources for research, technical assistance and transfer of technology to promote productive activities and industrialization.

11. To regulate aeronautic activity in the country's air space.

Article 317. The State will guarantee the creation, organization and performance of a participatory planning entity that includes representatives of public institutions and the organized civil society.

CHAPTER THREE

ECONOMIC POLICIES

Article 318.

I.   The State will determine the policy for industrial and commercial production that guarantees a sufficient supply of goods and services to adequately cover basic domestic needs, and the strengthening of export capacity.

II.   The State recognizes and will prioritize the support for the organization of associative structures of micro, small and medium productive enterprises, both urban and rural.

III.   The State will strengthen the productive, manufacturing and industrial infrastructure and basic services for the productive sector.

IV.   The State will prioritize the promotion of rural productive development as fundamental to the development policies of the country.

V.   The State will promote and support the export of value added goods and services.

Article 319.

I.   The industrialization of natural resources will be a priority in the economic policies, within the framework of respect for and protection of the environment and of the rights of the indigenous originary farmer nations and people and their territories. The articulation of the exploitation of natural resources with the internal productive apparatus will be a priority in the economic policies of the State.

II.   For the commercialization of strategic natural and energy resources, the State will consider, in order to define the commercialization price, the taxes, royalties and the corresponding participations that must be paid to the public treasury.

Article 320.

I.   Bolivian investment will take priority over foreign investment.

II.   Every foreign investment will be subjected to the Bolivian jurisdiction, laws and authorities, and no one may invoke an exceptional situation, nor appeal to diplomatic claims to obtain a more favorable treatment.

III.   The economic relations with foreign states or enterprises shall be conducted under conditions of independence, mutual respect and equity. More favorable conditions may not be granted to foreign States or enterprises than those established for Bolivians.

IV.   The State acts independently in all of its decisions on internal economic policy, and shall not accept demands or conditions imposed on this policy by states, banks or Bolivian or foreign financial institutions, multilateral entities or transnational enterprises.

V.   Public policies will promote internal consumption of products made in Bolivia.

SECTION I

FISCAL POLICY

Article 321.

I.   The economic and financial administration of the State and of all the public entities is governed by its budget.

II.   The determination of expenses and public investment will be made by means of participatory mechanisms involving the citizenry, technical planning and the state executive. The allocations shall attend especially to education, health, nutrition, housing and productive development.

III.   The Executive Organ will present to the Plurinational Legislative Assembly, at least two months before the end of each fiscal year, the proposed law for the General Budget for the following term, which will include all of the entities of the public sector.

IV.   Every bill that implies expenses or investments for the State must establish the source of funding, the way in which they will be covered, and the manner of its investment. If the bill was not presented by initiative of the Executive Organ, it requires a prior consultation with it.

V.   The Executive Organ, through the Ministry of the relevant branch, will have direct access to the information concerning the expenses that are budgeted and spent in every public sector. This access shall include information on the expenses budgeted and spent by the Armed Forces and the Bolivian Police.

Article 322.

I.   The Plurinational Legislative Assembly will authorize the contracting of public debt when the capacity to generate revenue to cover capital and interests is demonstrated, and when the most advantageous conditions of rates, payment schedules, amounts and other circumstances are technically justified.

II.   Public debt may not include obligations that have not been authorized and expressly guaranteed by the Plurinational Legislative Assembly.

Article 323.

I. The fiscal policy is based on the principles of economic capacity, equality, progressiveness, proportionality, transparency, universality, control, administrative simplicity and collection ability.

II. The taxes which belong to the national tax domain will be approved by the Plurinational Legislative Assembly. The taxes that belong to the exclusive domain of the departmental or municipal autonomies, will be approved, modified or eliminated by their Councils or Assemblies at the request of their executive organs. The tax domain of the Decentralized Departments, and regions will be conformed of departmental taxes, fees and special contributions, respectively.

III. The Plurinational Legislative Assembly by means of a law, will classify and define the taxes that belong to the national, departmental and municipal tax domains.

IV. The creation, suppression or modification of taxes under the dominion of the autonomous governments with such faculties will be conducted within the following limits:

1. No taxes may be created of which impositions are analogous to those corresponding to existing national taxes or other departmental or municipal taxes, independently of the tax domain to which they belong.

2. No taxes may be created that encumber goods, economic activity or patrimony outside of their territorial jurisdiction, except revenues generated by their citizens or enterprises outside of the country. This prohibition extends to fees, certificates and special contributions.

3. No taxes may be created that impede the free circulation and establishment of persons, assets, activities or services within the territorial jurisdiction. This prohibition extends to fees, certificates and special contributions.

4. No taxes may be created that generate privileges for residents in a discriminatory manner. This prohibition extends to fees, certificates and special contributions.

Article 324. The debts for economic damages caused to the State will never prescribe.

Article 325. Illicit economic activity, speculation, hoarding, usury, contraband, tax evasion and other related economic crimes will be punished by law.

SECTION II

MONETARY POLICY

Article 326.

I. The State, through the Executive Organ, will determine the goals of the monetary and exchange policies of the country in coordination with the Central Bank of Bolivia.

II. Public transactions in the country will be conducted in national currency.

Article 327. The Central Bank of Bolivia is an institution of public law, with its own legal personality and patrimony. Within the framework of the economic policy of the State, it is the function of the Central Bank of Bolivia to maintain the stability of the internal purchasing power of the currency in order to contribute to economic and social development.

Article 328.

I. In addition to what is set forth in the law, the attributions of the Central Bank of Bolivia, in coordination with the economic policy determined by the Executive Organ, are the following:

   1. To determine and execute the monetary policy.

   2. To execute the exchange policy.

   3. To regulate the system of payments.

   4. To authorize the issuance of currency.

   5. To manage the international reserves.

Article 329.

I. The Board of Directors of the Central Bank of Bolivia will be composed of a male or female President, and five male or female directors appointed by the male or female President of the State from lists of candidates presented by the Plurinational Legislative Assembly for each one of the positions.

II.   The members of the Board of Directors of the Central Bank of Bolivia will have terms of five years, and are not eligible for re-election. They will be considered public servants, in accordance to the Constitution and the law. The specific requisites for the position will be set forth by law.

III.   The members of the Board of Directors of the Central Bank of Bolivia will report and give accounts on the performance of the institution as often as requested by the Plurinational Legislative Assembly or its Chambers. The Central Bank of Bolivia will deliver an annual report to the Legislative Assembly and is subject to the governmental and fiscal system of control of the State.

SECTION III

FINANCIAL POLICY

Article 330.

I.   The State will regulate the financial system based on the criteria of equality of opportunity, solidarity, equitable distribution and redistribution.

II.   The State, through its financial policy, will prioritize the demand for financial services of the sectors of micro and small enterprises, artisans, commerce, service, community organizations and production cooperatives.

III.   The State will stimulate the creation of non-banking financial entities for the objective of socially productive investment.

IV.   The Central Bank of Bolivia and the public entities and institutions will not recognize the debts of private banks or financial entities. These banks and entities have the obligation to contribute to and strengthen a fund for financial restructuring, which will be used in cases of bank insolvency.

V.   The financial operations of the Public Administration, in its different levels of government, will be conducted by a public banking entity. The law will provide for its creation.

Article 331. The activities of financial intermediation, the rendering of financial services and any other activity related to the management, use and investment of savings, are matters of public interest and may only be exercised with prior authorization of the State, in accordance to law.

Article 332.

I. The financial entities will be regulated and supervised by an institution of banking and financial entity regulation. This institution will be of public law and will have jurisdiction in the entire territory of Bolivia.

II. The highest authority of the institution for banking and financial entity regulation will be appointed by the male or female President of the State from among a list of candidates proposed by the Plurinational Legislative Assembly, in accordance with the procedure established by law.

Article 333. The financial operations conducted by natural or legal persons, Bolivians or foreigners, will enjoy the right of confidentiality, except in judicial procedures, in cases of the alleged commission of financial crimes, in those in which fortunes are being investigated and in others defined by the law. The instances designated by law to investigate such cases will have the attribution to obtain information about such financial operations, without the need of judicial authorization.

SECTION IV

SECTOR POLICIES

Article 334. Within the framework of the policies of the sector, the State will protect and encourage:

1. The farmer economic organizations, and the associations or organizations of small urban producers, artisans, as supportive and reciprocal alternatives. The economic policy shall facilitate access to technical training and technology, to loans, to the opening of markets, and to the improvement of productive processes.

2. The guild sector, the self-employed, and retail commerce, in the areas of production, services and sales, shall be strengthened by means of access to credit and technical assistance.

3. The production of crafts with cultural identity.

4. The micro and small enterprises, as well as the farmer economic organizations, and organizations or associations of small producers, who will enjoy preference in the purchases of the State.

Article 335. The public service cooperatives will be organizations of collective interest, nonprofit seekers and subjected to governmental control, and they shall be administered democratically. The election of their administrative and supervisory authorities shall be conducted according to their own statutory norms and supervised by the Plurinational Electoral Organ. Their organization and operation will be regulated by law.

Article 336. The State will support communitarian economic organizations so that they may access credit and financing.

Article 337.

I.   Tourism is a strategic economic activity that must be developed in a sustainable manner that takes into account the respect for the treasures of the culture and the environment.

II.   The State shall promote and protect communitarian tourism with the objective of benefiting urban and rural communities, and the indigenous originary farmer nations and people where this activity is conducted.

Article 338. The State recognizes the economic value of housework as a source of wealth and it shall be quantified in public accounts.

CHAPTER FOUR

ASSETS AND RESOURCES OF THE STATE AND THEIR DISTRIBUTION

Article 339.

I.   The President of the Republic can decree payments that are not authorized by the budget law, only to attend to necessities that cannot be delayed arising from public calamities, internal disturbance or the exhaustion of resources destined to maintain services of which paralysis would cause serious harm. The expenses destined for these objectives will not exceed one percent of the total expenditures authorized by the General Budget.

II.   The assets that form part of the patrimony of the State and those of public entities are property of the Bolivian people, and are inviolable, non-attachable, imprescribable, and not subjected to expropriation; they may not be employed to the benefit of any individual. Their qualification, inventory, administration, disposition, mandatory registration and kinds of reivindications will be regulated by law.

III.   The income of the State will be invested in accordance to the general economic and social development plan of the country, the General Budget of the State and the law.

Article 340.

I.   The revenue of the State is divided into national, departmental, municipal and indigenous originary farmer and will be invested independently by their Treasuries, in accordance to their respective budgets.

II.   The law will classify the national, departmental, municipal and indigenous originary farmer income.

III.   The departmental, municipal, indigenous originary farmer autonomies, judicial and university resources collected by dependent offices of the national level, will not be centralized in the National Treasury.

IV.   The national Executive Organ will establish the norms for the elaboration and presentation of the proposed budgets of the entire public sector, including the autonomies.

Article 341. The following are departmental resources:

1.   The departmental royalties created by law.

2.   The participation in the revenue derived from taxes on Hydrocarbons according to the percentages set forth by law.

3.   Taxes, fees, special contributions and departmental certificates over natural resources.

4.   The transfers from the General Treasury of the Nation which are allocated to cover the expenses of personal health, education and social assistance.

5.   The extraordinary transfers of the General Treasury of the Nation, in the cases established in article 339.I of this Constitution.

6.   The internal and foreign credits and loans contracted in accordance to the norms of public debt and of the National system of Treasury and Public Credit.

7.   The income derived from the sale of goods, services and the sale of assets.

8.   Bequests, donations and other similar income.

TITLE II

ENVIRONMENT, NATURAL RESOURCES, LAND AND TERRITORY

CHAPTER ONE

ENVIRONMENT

Article 342. It is the duty of the State and the population to conserve, protect and use natural resources and biodiversity in a sustainable manner, as well as to maintain the equilibrium of the environment.

Article 343. The population has the right to participate in environmental management, and be consulted and informed prior to any decision that could affect the quality of the environment.

Article 344.

I. The manufacture and use of chemical, biological and nuclear weapons on Bolivian territory are prohibited, as well as the internment, transit and deposit of nuclear and toxic waste.

II. The State will regulate the internment, production, sale and employment of techniques, methods, supplies and substances that affect health and the environment.

Article 345. The policies of environmental management are based on the following:

1. Participatory planning and management, with social control.

2. The application of evaluation systems of environmental impact and control of the quality of the environment, without exception and in a way that includes all activity of production of goods and services that use, transform or affect natural resources and the environment.

3. Liability for executing any activity that produces environmental harm and civil, criminal and administrative sanctions for non-compliance with the norms for the protection of the environment.

Article 346. The natural assets are of public importance and of strategic character for the sustainable development of the country. Their conservation and use for the benefit of the population swill be the responsibility and exclusive authority of the State, and the sovereignty over natural resources may not be compromised. The law will establish the principles and provisions for their management.

Article 347.

I.   The State and society will promote the mitigation of the harmful effects on the environment and of the environmental pollution and damage that affects the country. Liability will be declared for damages to historic environments, and liability for environmental crimes will be imprescribable.

II.   Those who conduct activities that impact the environment must, at all stages of production, avoid, minimize, mitigate, remediate, repair and make compensation for the harms caused to the environment and the health of persons, and shall establish the security measures necessary to neutralize the possible effects of environmental pollution and damage.

CHAPTER TWO

NATURAL RESOURCES

Article 348.

I.   Minerals in all of their states, the hydrocarbons, water, air, soil and the subsoil, the forests, the biodiversity, the electromagnetic spectrum and all the elements and physical forces capable of use, are considered natural resources.

II.   The natural resources are of strategic character and of public importance for the development of the country.

Article 349.

I.   The natural resources are property and of direct domain, indivisible and without limitation, of the Bolivian people, and their administration corresponds to the State on behalf of the collective interest.

II.   The State will recognize, respect and grant individual and collective ownership rights over land, as well as rights of use and enjoyment of natural resources.

III.   Agriculture, stockbreeding, as well as the activities of hunting and fishing that do not involve protected animal species, are activities that are governed by what is established in the fourth part of this Constitution related to the economic organization and structure of the State.

Article 350. Any title granted over fiscal reserves shall be null and void, except by express authorization for state necessity and public utility, in accordance to law.

Article 351.

I.   The State, will assume control and direction of the exploration, exploitation, industrialization, transport and trade of strategic natural resources through public, cooperative or communitarian entities, which may in turn contract private enterprises and constitute mixed enterprises.

II. The State will subscribe contracts of association with legal persons, Bolivian or foreign, for the use of natural resources. Making sure of the reinvestment of the economic profits in the country.

III. The management and administration of natural resources will be conducted guaranteeing social participation and control within the design of the sector policies. Mixed enterprises may be established for the management and administration, with representation of the state and society, and safeguarding the collective welfare.

IV. Private enterprises, Bolivian or foreign, will pay taxes and royalties when they take part in the exploitation of natural resources, and the payments conducted will not be reimbursable. The royalties for the use of natural resources are a right and a compensation for their exploitation, and they will be regulated by the Constitution and the Law.

Article 352. The exploitation of natural resources in a determined territory will be subjected to a process of consultation with the affected population, called by the State, which will be free, prior in time and informed. Citizen participation is guaranteed in the process of management of the environment, and the conservation of ecosystems will be promoted, in accordance with the Constitution and the law. Within the indigenous originary farmer nations and people, the consultation will be conducted with respect given to their own norms and procedures.

Article 353. The Bolivian people will have equitable access to the benefits which come from the use of all the natural resources. Priority participation will be assigned to the territories where these resources are found, and to the indigenous originary farmer nations and people.

Article 354. The State will develop and promote research related to the management, conservation and use of natural resources and biodiversity.

Article 355.

I. The industrialization and sale of natural resources will be a priority of the State.

II. The profits obtained from the exploitation and sale of the natural resources will be distributed and reinvested to promote economic diversification in the different territorial levels of the State. The percentage distribution of profits will be approved by law.

III. The processes of industrialization will be conducted with preference given to the place of origin of the production and will create conditions that favor competitiveness in the internal and international market.

Article 356. The activities of exploration, exploitation, refining, industrialization, transportation and sale of non-renewable natural resources will have the character of state necessity and public utility.

Article 357. Because of being social property of the Bolivian people, no foreign person or enterprise, nor any private Bolivian person or enterprise, may register the property title to Bolivian natural resources in stock markets, nor can they use them as means for financial operations that grant title to or use them as security. The annotation and registry of reserves is the exclusive attribution of the State.

Article 358. The rights of use and exploitation of natural resources will be subjected to what is established in the Constitution and the law. These rights will be subjected to periodic review for compliance with the technical, economic and environmental regulations. The violation of the law will lead to the reversion or nullification of the rights of use and exploitation.

CHAPTER THREE

HYDROCARBONS

Article 359.

I. The hydrocarbons, in whatever state they are found or form in which they are, are the inalienable and unlimited property of the Bolivian people. The State, on behalf of and in representation of the Bolivian people, is the owner of the entire hydrocarbon production of the country and is the only one authorized to sell it. The totality of the income received by the sale of hydrocarbons will be the property of the State.

II. No contract, agreement or convention, of form, direct or indirect, tacit or express, can violate totally or partially what is established in this article.

In the event of violation, the contracts will be null and void as a matter of law, and those who have agreed to, signed, approved or executed them, have committed the crime of treason.

Article 360. The state will define the policy for hydrocarbons, will promote their comprehensive, sustainable and equitable development, and will guarantee energy sovereignty.

Article 361.

I. Yacimientos Petroliferos Fiscales Bolivianos (YPFB) is a self-sufficient enterprise of pubic law, non-attachable, with autonomy of administrative, technical and economic management, within the framework of the state hydrocarbon policy. YPFB, under the legal protection of the Ministry of the branch and as the operative arm of the State, is the only one authorized to conduct activities in the productive chain of hydrocarbons and their sale.

II. YPFB may not transfer its rights or obligations in any form or modality, whether tacit or express, direct or indirectly.

Article 362.

I. YPFB is authorized to sign contracts for services with public, mixed or private enterprises, Bolivian or foreign, so that said enterprises, in their name and representation, conducts determined activities in the productive chain in exchange for compensation or payment for their services. In no case may the signing of these contracts signify losses for YPFB or the State.

II. The contracts referring to activities of exploration and exploitation of hydrocarbons must have the prior authorization and express approval of the Plurinational Legislative Assembly. In the event this authorization is not obtained, they will be null and void as a matter of law, without the necessity of a judicial or extra-judicial declaration.

Article 363.

I. The Bolivian Enterprise of Hydrocarbon Industrialization (EBIH) is a self-sufficient public law enterprise, with autonomy in its administrative, technical and economic management, under the legal protection of the Ministry of the branch and YPFB, which acts in the area of state hydrocarbon policy. EBIH, in representation of the State and within its territory, will be responsible for conducting the industrialization of the hydrocarbons.

II. YPFB may form associations or mixed economic enterprises for the execution of the activities of exploration, exploitation, refining, industrialization, transport and sale of hydrocarbons. In these associations and companies, YPBF must have a shareholder participation of no less than fifty one percent of the total capital of the company.

Article 364. YPFB, on behalf and in representation of the Bolivian State, will operate and exercise property rights in the territories of other states.

Article 365. A self-sufficient institution of public law, with autonomy in its administrative, technical and economic management, under the legal protection of the Ministry of the branch, will be responsible for the regulations, control, supervision and fiscal control of the activities of the entire productive chain until industrialization, within the framework of the state hydrocarbons policy, in accordance to law.

Article 366. Every foreign enterprise that conducts activities in the productive chain of hydrocarbons in name and representation of the State will submit to the sovereignty of the State, and to the laws and authority of the State. No foreign court case or foreign jurisdiction will be recognized, and they may not invoke any exceptional situation for international arbitration, nor appeal to diplomatic claims.

Article 367. The exploitation, consumption and sale of hydrocarbons and its derivatives must be subjected to a policy of development that guarantees internal consumption. The export of the excess production will incorporate the greatest quantity of value added possible.

Article 368. The departments that are producers of hydrocarbons will receive a royalty of eleven percent of their audited departmental production of hydrocarbons. Similarly, the non-producer departments of hydrocarbons and the General Treasury of the State will obtain a participation in the percentages, which will be established by a special law.

CHAPTER FOUR

MINING AND METALLURGY

Article 369.

I.   The State will be responsible for the mineral riches that are found in the soil and subsoil whatever may be their origin and their application will be regulated by law. The private mining industry and cooperative companies are recognized as productive actors of the state mining industry.

II.   The nonmetallic natural resources existing in the salts, brines, evaporations, sulfurs and other substances, are of strategic character for the country.

III.   The direction of the mining and metallurgy policy is the responsibility of the State, as well as the encouragement, promotion and control of mining activity.

IV.   The State will exercise control of and audit the entire productive chain of mining and of the activities developed by the owners of mining rights, mining contracts or pre-existing rights.

Article 370.

I.   The State will grant mining rights in the entire productive chain, and it will sign mining contracts with individual and collective persons upon prior compliance with the norms established by law.

II.   The State will promote and strengthen cooperative mines so that they contribute to the social economic development of the country.

III.   The mining rights in the entire productive chain as well as in mining contracts must fulfill a social economic function, carried out directly by their titleholders.

IV.   The mining right which includes the investments and works of prospecting, exploration, exploitation, concentration, industrialization or sale of minerals and metals is the domain of the titleholders. The law will define the reach of this right.

V.   The mining contract will obligate the beneficiaries to develop mining activities to satisfy the social economic interest. The failure to fulfill this obligation will lead to the immediate dissolution of the contract.

VI.   The State, through self-sufficient entities, will promote and develop policies for the administration, prospecting, exploration, exploitation, industrialization, commercialization, and for technical, geological and scientific information and evaluation of non-renewable natural resources for mining development.

Article 371.

I.   The areas of mining exploitation granted by contract are non-transferable, non- attachable, and cannot pass by hereditary succession.

II.   The legal domicile of the mining enterprises will be established in the local jurisdiction where the greatest amount of mining exploitation is conducted.

Article 372.

I.   Belong to the people's patrimony, the nationalized mining groups, their industrial plants and their foundries, which cannot be transferred or adjudicated as property of private enterprises pursuant to any title.

II.   The high level direction and administration of the mining industry will be entrusted to a self-sufficient entity with the attributions determined by law.

III.   The State will participate in the industrialization and sale of mineralogical, metallic and non-metallic resources, regulated by law.

IV.   The new self-sufficient enterprises created by the State shall establish their legal domicile in the departments of greatest mining production, Potosí and Oruro.

CHAPTER FIVE

WATER RESOURCES

Article 373.

I.   Water constitutes a fundamental right for life, within the framework of the sovereignty of the people. The State will promote the use and access to water on the basis of principles of solidarity, complementariness, reciprocity, equity, diversity and sustainability.

II.   Water resources in all their states, surface and subterraneous, constitute finite, vulnerable, strategic resources, and serve a social, cultural and environmental function. These resources cannot be the object of private appropriation and they, as well as water services, will not be given as concessions and are subjected to a system of licensing, registration and authorization in accordance to Law.

Article 374.

I.   The State will protect and guarantee the priority use of water for life. It is the duty of the State to manage, regulate, protect and plan the adequate and sustainable use of water resources, with social participation, guaranteeing access to water for all the inhabitants. The law will establish the conditions and limitations of all its uses.

II.   The State will recognize, respect and protect the uses and customs of the community, of its local authorities and the indigenous originary farmer nations and people over the right, management and administration of sustainable water.

III.   Fossil, glacial, wetland, subterraneous, mineral, medicinal and other waters are priorities for the State, which must guarantee their conservation, protection, preservation, restoration, sustainable use and complete management; they are inalienable, non-attachable and cannot be imprescribable.

Article 375.
I.   It is the duty of the State to develop plans for the use, conservation, management and sustainable exploitation of the river basins.

II.   The State will regulate the management and sustainable administration of the water resources and the basins for irrigation, food security and basic services, respecting the uses and customs of the communities.

III.   It is the duty of the State to conduct the studies for the identification of fossil waters and their consequent protection, management and sustainable use.

Article 376. Water resources coming from rivers, lakes and lagoons that form water basins are considered strategic resources for the development and sovereignty of Bolivia because of their potential, for the variety of natural resources that they contain, and because they are a fundamental part of the ecosystems. The State will avoid actions in the sources and intermediary zones of rivers that may cause damages to the ecosystems or diminish the flow volume, will preserve the natural state, and will watch over the development and wellbeing of the population.

Article 377.
I.   Every international treaty on water resources that the State signs will guarantee the sovereignty of the country and will prioritize the interests of the State.

II.   The State will safeguard permanently the border and transborder waters for the conservation of the water riches that contribute to the integration of the people.

CHAPTER SIX

ENERGY

Article 378.
I.   The different forms of energy and their sources constitute a strategic resource, its access is a fundamental and essential right for the integral and social development of the country, and will be governed by the

principles of efficiency, continuity, adaptability, and environmental preservation.

II.   It is the exclusive faculty of the State to develop the chain of energy production in the phases of generation, transport, and distribution, by means of public, mixed enterprises, non-profit institutions, cooperatives, private enterprises, and communitarian and social enterprises, with public participation and control. The chain of energy production may not be held exclusively by private interests, nor may it be licensed. Private participation will be regulated by law.

Article 379.

I.   The State will develop and promote research, as well as the use of new forms of production of alternative energy, compatible with the conservation of the environment.

II.   The State will guarantee the generation of energy for internal consumption; the export of excess energy must anticipate the reserves necessary for the country.

CHAPTER SEVEN

BIODIVERSITY, COCA, PROTECTED AREAS AND FORESTRY RESOURCES

SECTION I

BIODIVERSITY

Article 380.

I.   The renewable natural resources will be used in a sustainable way, respecting the characteristics and natural value of each ecosystem.

II.   In order to guarantee ecological equilibrium, the land must be used in accordance with its capacity for greater use within the framework of the process of the organization of use and occupation of lands, taking into account their biophysical, socioeconomic, and cultural characteristics, and institutional policies.

Article 381.

I.   Native species of animal and vegetable origin are natural assets. The State will establish the necessary measures for their conservation, exploitation and development.

II.   The State will protect all genetic and micro-organic resources which are found in the ecosystems of the territory, as well as the knowledge associated with their use and exploitation. For their protection a system of registry that safeguards their existence will be established, as well as a registry of the intellectual property in the name of the State or the local individuals who claim it. For all the resources not registered, the State will establish procedures for their protection with a law.

Article 382. It is the faculty and the duty of the State to defend, recover, protect and repatriate biological material derived from natural resources, from ancestral knowledge and other sources that originate in the territory.

Article 383. The State will establish measures for the partial or total, temporary or permanent, restriction of the uses of extracts from the resources of biodiversity. The measures will be oriented towards the need to preserve, conserve, recover and restore the biodiversity at risk of extinction. Illegal possession, handling and trafficking of biodiversity species will be criminally sanctioned.

SECTION II

COCA

Article 384. The State protects the originary and ancestral coca as cultural patrimony, as a renewable natural resource of the biodiversity of Bolivia, and as a factor of social unity; in its natural state it is not a narcotic. The reevaluation, production, sale and industrialization of coca will be governed by law.

SECTION III

PROTECTED AREAS

Article 385.

I. The protected areas constitute a common good, and they form part of the natural and cultural patrimony of the country; they perform environmental, cultural, social and economic functions for sustainable development.

II. Wherever indigenous originary farmer protected areas and territories overlap, shared management will be undertaken, subject to the norms and procedures of the indigenous originary farmer nations and people, respecting the objective of creation of these areas.

SECTION IV

FORESTRY RESOURCES

Article 386. The natural forests and forestry soils are of strategic character for the development of the Bolivian people. The State will recognize the rights to use the forests for the benefit of communities and individual operators. Likewise, it will promote activities of conservation and sustainable use, the generation of added value for its products, and the rehabilitation and reforestation of degraded areas.

Article 387.

I. The State will guarantee the conservation of natural forests in forestry areas, their sustainable exploitation, and the conservation and recovery of the flora, fauna, and degraded areas.

II. The law will regulate the protection and use of forestry species that have socio-economic, cultural and ecological relevance.

Article 388. The indigenous originary farmer communities located within forest areas will have the exclusive right to their use and their management, in accordance with the law.

Article 389.

I. The conversion of forest covered land to agricultural and other uses, will only be conducted in areas legally allocated for that use, in accordance with the planning policies and the law.

II. The law will determine the ecological rights of way and zoning of internal uses in order to guarantee the long term conservation of the land and bodies of water.

III.   All conversions of land in areas not classified for such purposes will constitute a punishable infraction and shall give rise to the obligation to repair the caused damages.

CHAPTER EIGHT

AMAZONIA

Article 390.

I.   The Bolivian Amazonia basin constitutes a strategic space of special protection for the integral development of the country due to its high environmental sensitivity, existing biodiversity, water resources and for the eco-regions.

II.   The Bolivian Amazonia includes the entire Department of Pando, Iturralde Province of the Department of La Paz and the provinces of Vaca Diez and Ballivan of the Department of Beni. The full development of the Bolivian Amazonia, as a territorial area of tropical rainforests, in accordance with the specific characteristics of the extract and harvesting resources, will be governed by a special law in benefit of the region and the country.

Article 391.

I.   The State will prioritize the sustainable, integral development of the Bolivian Amazonia, through a comprehensive, participatory, shared and equitable administration of the Amazon jungle. The administration will be directed to the generation of employment and the improvement of the income of its inhabitants, within the framework of protection and sustainability of the environment.

II.   The State will encourage access to financing for tourism, eco-tourism and other initiatives of regional entrepreneurship.

III.   The State in coordination with the indigenous originary farmer authorities and the inhabitants of the Amazonia, will create a special, decentralized organ, headquartered in the Amazonia, to promote its own activities within the region.

Article 392.

I.   The State will implement special policies in benefit of the indigenous originary farmer nations and people of the region in order to generate the necessary conditions for the reactivation, encouragement, industrialization, commercialization, protection and conservation of traditional extract products.

II.   The historical cultural and economic value of the siringa and the castaño is recognized, symbols of the Bolivian Amazonia, of which cutting will be sanctioned, except in the cases of public interest as regulated by law.

CHAPTER NINE

LAND AND TERRITORY

Article 393. The State recognizes, protects and guarantees individual and communitarian or collective property of land, as long as it fulfills a social purpose or social economic purpose, as the case may be.

Article 394.

I.   Individual agrarian property is classified as small, medium and corporate, in function to its surface area, the production, and the development criteria. Its maximum and minimum extensions, characteristics and forms of conversion will be regulated by law. Legally acquired rights by individual owners, whose piece of land is inside indigenous originary farmer territories, are guaranteed.

II.   The small property is indivisible, it constitutes a family asset that is non-attachable, and it is not subject to agrarian property taxes. The indivisibility does not affect the right of hereditary succession under the conditions established by law.

III.   The State recognizes, protects and guarantees communitarian or collective property, which includes indigenous originary farmer territory, native, intercultural communities and rural communities. Collective property is declared indivisible, imprescribable, non-attachable, inalienable and irreversible, and will not be subjected to agrarian property taxes. Communities can be titleholders, recognizing the complementary character of collective and individual rights, respecting territorial unity with identity.

Article 395.

I.   Fiscal lands will be granted to indigenous originary farmer people, intercultural indigenous communities, afro-Bolivians and farmer communities which do not possess them or that are insufficient, in accordance with a State policy concerned with the ecological and geographic realities, as well as the population, social, cultural and economic necessities. The granting will be conducted according to the policies of sustainable rural development and the right of women to access, distribution and redistribution of land, without discrimination based on civil status or marital union.

II. Double grantings, purchase and sale, exchange and donation of granted lands are prohibited.

III. For being contrary to collective interest, the obtaining of income generated by the speculative use of the land is prohibited.

Article 396.

I. The State will regulate the land market, preventing the accumulation in surface areas greater than what is recognized by law, as well as its division into surface areas less than what is established for the small property.

II. Male or female foreigners may not acquire lands of the State under any title.

Article 397.

I. Labor is the fundamental source for the acquisition and maintenance of agrarian property. Properties must be used to serve a social purpose or a social economic purpose in order to safeguard their right, depending on the nature of the property.

II. Social purpose will be understood as the sustainable use of the land by the indigenous originary farmer communities, as well as that conducted in small properties, and it constitutes the source of subsistence and wellbeing and sociocultural development of its titleholders. The norms of the communities are recognized in the fulfillment of the social purpose.

III. The social economic purpose must be understood as the sustainable employment of the land within the development of productive activities, in accordance to its capacity of greater use, in benefit of society, of the collective interest and of its owner. The corporate property is subjected to review in accordance to law, to verify the compliance with the social economic purpose.

Article 398. Latifundio and double titles are prohibited for being contrary to the collective interest and the development of the country. Latifundio is understood to mean the non-productive holding of land; the land that does not fulfill a social economic function; the exploitation of land that applies a system of servitude, almost-slavery and slavery in labor relations or the property that surpasses the maximum zoned surface area established by law. In no case may the maximum surface exceed five thousand hectares.

Article 399.

I.   The new limits of zoned agrarian property will be applied to pieces of land that have been acquired after this Constitution enters into force. For purposes of the non-retroactivity of the Law, the rights of possession and agrarian property are recognized and respected in accordance to Law.

II. The surface areas exceeding those that fulfill the Social Economic Purpose will be expropriated. The double titles set forth in the prior article refers to the double grantings processed before the ex-National Council of Agrarian Reform, CNRA. The prohibition of double grantings is not applied to legally acquired rights of third parties.

Article 400. Because of affecting sustainable use and for being contrary to the collective interest, the division of land into areas less than the maximum area of the small property as recognized in the law is prohibited. The maximum area for a small property established by law will take into account the characteristics of the geographic zone. The State will establish legal mechanisms to avoid the division of the small property.

Article 401.

I.   The failure to fulfill the social economic purpose or the holding of latifundio will result in the reversion of the land, and the land will pass into the domain and property of the Bolivian people.

II. The expropriation of land will occur for reasons of necessity and public utility and upon prior payment of a fair indemnity.

Article 402. The State has the obligation to:

1.   Encourage plans for human settlement to achieve a rational demographic distribution and better use of the land and natural resources, granting to new settlements the facilities to have access to education, health, food security and production, within the framework of the Territorial Organization of the State and the conservation of the environment.

2.   Promote policies aimed at eliminating all forms of discrimination against women in the access, ownership and inheritance of land.

Article 403.

I.   The totality of the indigenous originary farmer territory is recognized, which includes the right to its land, to the use and exclusive utilization of the renewable natural resources under the conditions determined by law; to prior and informed consultation and to participation in the benefits of the exploitation of the non-renewable natural resources that are found in their territories; to the authority to apply their own norms, administered by their structures of representation, and to define their development in accordance to their own cultural criteria and principles of harmonious coexistence with nature. The indigenous originary farmer territories can be composed of communities.

II.   The indigenous originary farmer territory includes areas of production, areas of use and conservation of natural resources and spaces for social, spiritual and cultural reproduction. The law will establish the procedure for the recognition of these rights.

Article 404. The Agrarian Reform Service of Bolivia, of which highest authority is the President of the State, is the entity responsible for planning, executing and consolidating the agrarian reform process and has jurisdiction in the entire territory of the country.

TITLE III

COMPREHENSIVE SUSTAINABLE RURAL DEVELOPMENT

Article 405. The comprehensive sustainable rural development is a fundamental part of the economic policies of the State, which will prioritize its actions to encourage all communitarian economic undertakings and those of rural actors, placing emphasis on food security and sovereignty, by means of the following:

1.   The sustained and sustainable increase of agricultural, livestock, manufacturing, agro-industrial, and tourist industry productivity, as well as their commercial competitiveness capacity.

2.   The articulation and internal complementarity of the structures of the agricultural, livestock and agro-industrial production.

3.   The achievement of better conditions for economic exchange of the rural productive sector in relation to the rest of the Bolivian economy.

4.   The significance and respect of the indigenous originary farmer communities in all dimensions of their life.

5.   The strengthening of the economy of the small agricultural and livestock producers and of the family and communitarian economy.

Article 406.

I.   The State will guarantee the sustainable comprehensive rural development by means of policies, plans, programs and comprehensive projects that encourage agricultural, artisan, and forestry production, and tourism, with the goal of obtaining a better use, transformation, industrialization and commercialization of renewable natural resources.

II.   The State will promote and strengthen the rural economic productive organizations, among which are the artisans, the cooperatives, the associations of agricultural producers and manufacturers, and the micro, small and medium communitarian agricultural enterprises, which contribute to the social economic development of the country, in accordance with their cultural and productive identity.

Article 407. The objectives of the State policy for comprehensive rural development, in coordination with the autonomous and decentralized territorial entities, are the following:

1.   To guaranty food security and sovereignty, prioritizing the production and consumption of agricultural foods produced in the Bolivian territory.

2.   To establish mechanisms for the protection of Bolivian agricultural production.

3.   To promote the production and sale of agro ecological products.

4.   To protect the agricultural and agro-industrial production against natural disasters and climatic, geological and sinister catastrophes. The law will provide for the creation of an agricultural insurance.

5.   To implement and develop technical, productive, and ecological education, at all levels and in all modalities.

6.   To establish policies and sustainable projects, seeking the conservation and recuperation of the soils.

7.   To promote irrigation systems for the purpose of guaranteeing agricultural and livestock production.

8.   To guarantee technical assistance and the establishment of mechanisms of innovation and transfer of technology in the entire agricultural productive chain.

9.   To establish the creation of a seed bank and centers of genetic research.

10.   To establish policies to encourage and support the productive agricultural sectors that have natural structural weaknesses.

11.   To control the exit and entrance into the country of biological and genetic resources.

12.   To establish policies and programs to guarantee agricultural sanitation and food safety.

13.   To provide productive, manufacturing and industrial infrastructure and basic services for the agricultural sector.

Article 408. The State will determine the incentives in benefit of small and medium producers for the purpose of compensating for the disadvantages of unequal exchange between agricultural and livestock products with the rest of the economy.

Article 409. The production, import and trade of genetically altered products will be regulated by law.

FIFTH PART

NORMATIVE HIERARCHY AND CONSTITUTIONAL REFORM

SOLE TITLE

SUPREMACY AND REFORM OF THE CONSTITUTION

Article 410.

I.   All persons, natural and legal, as well as public organs, public functions and institutions, are subjected to the Constitution herein.

II.   The Constitution is the supreme norm of Bolivian law and enjoys supremacy before any other normative provision. The constitutional legislation includes the international Treaties and Conventions in the matter of human rights and the norms of Communitarian Law, ratified by the country. The application of the legal norms will be governed by the following hierarchy, in accordance with the competences of the territorial entities:

1.   The Political Constitution of the State

2.   The international treaties

3.   The national laws, autonomic statutes, organic charters and the other departmental, municipal and indigenous legislation.

4.   Decrees, regulations and other resolutions issued by the corresponding executive organs.

Article 411.

I.   The total reform of the Constitution, or that which affects its fundamental bases, the rights, duties and guarantees, or the supremacy and reform of the Constitution, will take place through an originary plenipotentiary Constituent Assembly, activated by popular will through referendum. The calling for the referendum will be conducted by citizen initiative, with the signatures of at least twenty percent of the electorate; by absolute majority vote of the members of the Plurinational Legislative Assembly; or by the male or female President of the State. The Constituent Assembly will draft its own regulations for all effects, having to approve the constitutional text by two thirds of the total of its members present. The validity of the reform will require its approval by constitutional referendum.

II.   The partial reform of the Constitution may be initiated by popular initiative, with the signatures of at least twenty percent of the electorate, or by the Plurinational Legislative Assembly through a law of constitutional reform approved by two thirds of the total members present of the Plurinational Legislative Assembly. Any partial reform will require approval by constitutional referendum.

TRANSITORY DISPOSITIONS

First.

I.   Within a term of 60 days from the enactment of the Constitution herein, the Congress of the Republic will approve a new electoral regime for the election of the Plurinational Legislative Assembly, the President, and Vice-President of the Republic; the election will take place on December 6th, 2009.

II.   The previous mandates to the time this Constitution enters into effect will be taken into account for purposes of computing the new terms of office.

III.   The elections of departmental and municipal authorities will take place on April 4th, 2010.

IV.   Exceptionally, the mandates of the Mayors, Municipal Councils and Prefects of the Departments will be extended until the appointment of the newly elected authorities in accordance to the previous paragraph.

Second. The Plurinational Legislative Assembly will approve, within the maximum term of one hundred and eighty days from the time of its installation, the Law of the Plurinational Electoral Organ, the Law of the Judicial Organ, the Law of the Plurinational Constitutional Court, and the Autonomies and Decentralization Framework Law.

Third.
I.   The departments that opted for departmental autonomy in the referendum of July 2nd, 2006, will access directly to the regime of departmental autonomy, in accordance to the Constitution.

II.   The departments that opted for departmental autonomy in the referendum of July 2nd, 2006, must adjust their statutes to this Constitution and subject them to constitutional control.

Fourth. The election of the authorities of the organs included in the second provision, will be conducted in conformity with the electoral calendar established by the Plurinational Electoral Organ.

Fifth. During the first mandate of the Plurinational Legislative Assembly the laws necessary for the development of the constitutional provisions will be approved.

Sixth. Within the maximum term of one year after the Law of the Judicial Organ enters into effect, and in accordance thereto, the judicial positions will be reviewed.

Seventh. For purposes of application of paragraph I of article 293 of this Constitution, the indigenous territory will have as the basis of its demarcation the Communitarian Lands of Origin. Within the term of one year from the election of the Executive and Legislative Organ, the category of Communitarian Land of Origin will be subjected to administrative process for its conversion to Indigenous Originary Farmer Territory, within the framework established in this Constitution.

Eight.
I.   In the period of one year from the election of the Executive Organ and the Legislative Organ, the concessions over natural resources, electricity, telecommunications and basic services must adjust to the new legal system. In no case shall the migration of the concessions to the new legal system signify the failure to recognize acquired rights.

II.   In the same period, the mining concessions of metallic and non-metallic minerals, crystals, salts, sulfur and others, granted in the fiscal reserves of Bolivian territory, will cease to be in effect.

III.   The mining concessions granted to national and foreign enterprises prior to the enactment of this Constitution, within a term of one year, must adjust thereto, through mining contracts.

IV.   The State recognizes and respects the pre-existing rights of the cooperative mining companies, for their social productive character.

V.   The concessions over radioactive minerals granted prior to the enactment of the Constitution are resolved, and are reverted to the State.

Ninth. The international treaties existing prior to the Constitution which do not contradict it, will be maintained in the internal legal order, with the rank of law. Within the period of four years after the election of the new Executive Organ, the Executive shall denounce and, in its case, renegotiate the international treaties that may be contrary to the Constitution.

Tenth. The requisite of speaking at least two official languages for the performance of public functions, as determined in Article 234.7, will be applied progressively in accordance to law.

ABROGATORY DISPOSITION

Abrogatory provision. The Constitution of the State of 1967 and its subsequent reforms is abrogated.

FINAL DISPOSITION

This Constitution, approved in referendum by the Bolivian people will enter into effect the day of its publication in the Official Gazette.

Remit it to the Executive Organ, for Constitutional purposes.

Therefore, I enact it to have it and comply with it as the fundamental Law of the new Social Unitary State of Plurinational Communitarian Law, decentralized and with autonomies.

City of El Alto of La Paz, on the seventh day of the month of February of the year two thousand and nine.

SIGNED. EVO MORALES AYMA
CONSTITUTIONAL PRESIDENT OF THE REPUBLIC

LAW AGAINST CORRUPTION, ILLICIT ENRICHMENT AND INVESTIGATION OF FORTUNES "MARCELO QUIROGA SANTA CRUZ"

As published by the *Gaceta Oficial de Bolivia* on March 2010.

LAW N° 004
DATED MARCH 31ST OF 2010

EVO MORALES AYMA
PRESIDENT OF THE PLURINATIONAL STATE OF BOLIVIA

For which, the Plurinational Legislative Assembly, has sanctioned the following Law:

THE PLURINATIONAL LEGISLATIVE ASSEMBLY

DECREES:

LAW AGAINST CORRUPTION, ILLICIT ENRICHMENT AND INVESTIGATION OF FORTUNES "MARCELO QUIROGA SANTA CRUZ"

CHAPTER I
GENERAL DISPOSITIONS

ARTICLE 1. (Objective). The Law herein has the objective of establishing the mechanisms and procedures within the framework of the Political Constitution of the State, the laws, treaties and the international conventions, in order to prevent, investigate, process and sanction any act of corruption perpetrated by public servants and ex public servants while in exercise of their functions, and by natural or juridical persons and legal representatives of juridical persons, public or private, national or foreign that compromise or affect the resources of the State, as well as for recovering the affected patrimony of the State through the competent judicial bodies.

ARTICLE 2. (Definition of Corruption). It is the direct or indirect requirement or acceptance, offering or granting, from a public servant or from a national or foreign natural or juridical person, of any pecuniary object of value or other benefits such as gifts, favors, promises or advantages for oneself or for another person or entity, in exchange of an action or omission of the conduction of any act that affects the interests of the State.

ARTICLE 3. (Purpose). The Law herein has the purpose of preventing and ending impunity within the acts of corruption, providing an effective fight against illicit enrichment, through the recovery and protection of the State's patrimony, with the active participation of the public and private entities and the civil society.

ARTICLE 4. (Principles). The principles that govern the Law herein are:

'Suma Qamaña' (Living Well). When there is a complementarity between the access to, and enjoyment of material properties, with affective, subjective and spiritual realization, everything in harmony with nature and in community with the human race.

'Ama Suwa' (Don't Be a Thief), **'Uhua'na machapi'tya'** (Don't Steal). Any national or foreign person must watch over the property and patrimony of the State; they have the obligation of protecting and guarding both as if their own, in benefit of the common good.

Ethics. It is the behavior of a person in accordance to the moral principles of community service, reflected in the values of honesty, transparency, integrity, probity, responsibility and efficiency.

Transparency. It is the practice and visible management of the resources of the State by public servants, as well as by natural or juridical persons, national or foreign that render services for or compromise the resources of the State.

Gratuity. The investigation and administration of justice within issues related to the fight against corruption, shall gave a gratuitous character.

Expeditiousness. The mechanism of investigation and administration of justice within issues related to the fight against corruption must be conducted in a prompt and timely manner.

The Defense of the Patrimony of the State. It is governed by the constitutional obligation that any Bolivian has to protect and guard the patrimony of the State, denouncing all acts or events of corruption.

Ample Cooperation. All entities that have the mission of fighting against corruption shall cooperate mutually, working in a coordinated manner exchanging information without restriction.

Impartiality in the Administration of Justice. All Bolivians have the right to a prompt, effective and transparent administration of justice.

ARTICLE 5. (Scope of Application).

I.   The Law herein applies to:

1)   The public servants and ex-servants of all the entities of the Plurinational State, its bodies and institutions at a central, decentralized or deconcentrated level, and of the autonomous, departmental, municipal, regional and indigenous originary farmer territories.

2)   The Public Ministry, the Office of the Attorney General of the State, the office of the Public Defender, the Central Bank of Bolivia, the office of the General Controller of the State, the Universities and the other entities that belong to the structure of the State.

3)   The Armed Forces and the Bolivian Police.

4)   The entities and organizations in which the State has a stock participation, independently from its juridical nature.

5)   The private persons, natural or juridical and all those persons who are not public servants but commit corruption crimes that cause economic damage to the State or that are unduly benefitted from its resources.

II.   The Law herein, in accordance to the Political Constitution of the State, does not recognize immunity, advantage or privilege of any kind, having to be of preferential application.

CHAPTER II

OF THE ENTITIES IN CHARGE OF FIGHTING AGAINST CORRUPTION

ARTICLE 6. (National Council for the Fight Against Corruption, Illicit Enrichment and Legitimization of Unlawful Earnings).

I.   The National Council for the Fight Against Corruption, Illicit Enrichment and Legitimization of Unlawful Earnings is created, being comprised of:

a)   The Ministry of Institutional Transparency and Fight Against Corruption.

b)   The Ministry of Government.

c)   The Public Ministry.

d)   The General Controller of the State.

e)   The Financial Investigation Unit.

f)   The Attorney General of the State.

g)   Representatives of the Organized Civil Society, in accordance to what is established in articles 241 and 242 of the Political Constitution of the State and the Law.

II.   The National Council for the Fight Against Corruption, Illicit Enrichment and Legitimization of Unlawful Earnings, will be presided by the representative of the Ministry of Institutional Transparency and Fight Against Corruption.

The entities that make up the Council are independent in the compliance of their specific attributions within the framework of the Political Constitution of the State and the laws.

III.   The National Council for the Fight Against Corruption, Illicit Enrichment and Legitimization of Unlawful Earnings, shall meet in an ordinary manner at least four times per year and extraordinarily when called by four of its members.

ARTICLE 7. (Attributions of the National Council for the Fight Against Corruption, Illicit Enrichment and Legitimization of Unlawful Earnings). The attributions of the National Council for the Fight Against Corruption, Illicit Enrichment and Legitimization of Unlawful Earnings are the following:

1)   To propose, supervise and monitor public policies, oriented towards preventing and sanctioning acts of corruption, in order to protect and recover the patrimony of the State.

2)   To approve the National Plan for the Fight Against Corruption, prepared by the relevant Ministry, responsible for these functions.

3)   To evaluate the execution of the National Plan for the Fight Against Corruption.

4)   To relate with the autonomous governments in what concerns to their attributions, in accordance with the provisions established in the Autonomies and Decentralization Framework Law.

ARTICLE 8. (Obligation of the National Council for the Fight Against Corruption, Illicit Enrichment and Legitimization of Unlawful Earnings to Inform its Results). The National Council for the Fight Against Corruption, Illicit Enrichment and Legitimization of Unlawful Earnings has the obligation of informing every year to the President of the Plurinational State, to the Plurinational Legislative Assembly and to the Organized Civil Society, the goals and results obtained during the execution of the National Plan for the Fight Against Corruption.

ARTICLE 9. (Social Control). In accordance to the Political Constitution of the State, Social Control will be exercised to prevent and fight against corruption. All social actors in an individual and/or collective manner can participate in the social control.

ARTICLE 10. (Rights and Attributions of Social Control). In an enunciatively but not limitative manner, the following are the rights and attributions of the Social Control:

a) To identify and denounce events of corruption before the competent authorities.

b) To identify and denounce the lack of transparency before the competent authorities.

c) To cooperate within administrative and judicial processes, for events or crimes of corruption.

ARTICLE 11. (Anti-Corruption Courts and Tribunals).

I.   The Anti-Corruption Courts and Tribunals are created, which will have the competence to know and resolve the penal processes regarding corruption matters and linked crimes, everything within a frame of respect for legal pluralism.

II.   The Judiciary Council will appoint in each department the number of judges necessary to know and resolve the processes, in accordance to the Political Constitution of the State.

ARTICLE 12. (Specialized Anti-Corruption Prosecutors). The General Prosecutor of the State, in accordance to the Organic Law of the Public Ministry, will appoint in each Department the specialized prosecutors that will be exclusively dedicated to the investigation and accusation of acts of the corruption and the linked crimes.

ARTICLE 13. (Specialized Investigators of the Bolivian Police). The Bolivian Police will have specialized anti-corruption investigators, within a Division for the Fight Against Corruption in each Department, who will exercise their functions under the functional direction of the prosecutors.

ARTICLE 14. (Obligation to be an Accusing Party). The maximum executive authority of the affected entity or the authority called for by the Law, shall mandatorily become an accusing party against the corruption and the linked crimes, once these are known, having to promote the corresponding legal actions before the competent authorities. Its omission will result in incurring in the crime of breach of duties and others that correspond, in accordance to the Law herein.

ARTICLE 15. (Indigenous Originary Farmer Jurisdiction). The application of the indigenous originary farmer jurisdiction will be governed as set forth in Articles 190, 191 and 192 of the Political Constitution of the State and the Law of Jurisdictional Demarcation.

ARTICLE 16. (Permanent Evaluation System). The specialized judges, prosecutors and police members will be subjected to a permanent evaluation system implemented in each entity, taking into account the guidelines established by the National Council for the Fight Against Corruption, Illicit Enrichment and Legitimization of Unlawful Earnings, to guaranty the probity and efficiency in the compliance of their functions. The Social Control will participate in this evaluation system.

ARTICLE 17. (Protection of Accusers and Witnesses).

I. The System of Protection for Accusers and Witnesses is established being at the charge of the Ministry of Government, the Bolivian Police and the Public Ministry, in accordance to regulation.

II. The System will provide adequate protection against any threat, aggression, retaliation or intimidation for accusers and witnesses, as well as for experts, technical advisors, public servants and other direct or indirect participants in the process of investigation, prosecution, accusation and judgment.

III.   The Ministry of Institutional Transparency and Fight Against Corruption, will maintain reserve regarding the identity of the individuals and public servants who denounce acts and/or crimes of corruption and will maintain in reserve the presented documentation, gathered and generated during the compliance of their functions.

IV.   In case of pronouncing an absolutory sentence, in accordance to section 3) of Article 363 of the Penal Procedure Code, after its execution, the jurisdictional instance that had the initial knowledge of the process, at a request of the interested party will lift the reserve of identity within a term of 72 hours; without prejudice to the defendant initiating a recriminatory action against the plaintiff in the penal action.

ARTICLE 18. (Attributions of the Financial Investigations Unit). Aside from those established by the Law, the Financial Investigations Unit shall have the following attributions:

1)   After written request by the Ministry of Transparency and Fight Against Corruption, the Attorney General of the State and/or the Anti-Corruption Prosecutors, or sua sponte, to analyze and conduct activities of financial and patrimonial intelligence, to identify presumptive corruption acts or crimes.

2)   To remit the results of the analysis and background to the Ministry of Institutional Transparency and Fight Against Corruption, the Attorney General of the State, the Public Ministry and the competent jurisdictional authority, when it corresponds.

ARTICLE 19. (Exemption of Secret or Confidentiality).

I.   Secret or confidentiality cannot be invoked in securities and guarantees, commercial, tax and economic matters when the Financial Investigations Unit, the Ministry of Institutional Transparency and Fight Against Corruption, the Public Ministry and the Attorney General of the State require information for the compliance of their functions; this information will be obtained without the need of a judicial order, a prosecutor requirement or any other prior process.

II.   The information obtained can only be used for the purpose of investigating corruption and other linked crimes, and will be free from the payment of any judicial or administrative charge.

ARTICLE 20. (Exemption of the Banking Secret for the Investigation of Corruption Crimes).

I.   There is no confidentiality within financial operations conducted by natural or juridical persons, Bolivian or foreign, in judicial processes, in cases where there is a presumption of the commission of financial crimes, in which fortunes are being investigated, in which crimes of corruption are being investigated and in processes of recovery of properties defrauded from the State.

II.   Public servants can waive the banking secret in a voluntary manner. The conducted waiver will have no effect when the public servant ceases its functions.

ARTICLE 21. (Duty to Report).

I.   The entities and subjects dedicated to the following activities have the duty to remit to the Financial Investigations Unit the requested information in case of an investigation:

a)   Purchase and sale of firearms, vehicles, metals, works of art, postal stamps and archeological objects;

b)   Trade of jewelry, precious stones and coins;

c)   Games of chance, casinos, lotteries and bingos;

d)   Hotel activities, tourism and travel agencies;

e)   Activities related with the productive chain of strategic natural resources;

f)   Activities related with the construction of highways and/or road infrastructure;

g)   Customs clearers, and import and export companies;

h)   Non-Governmental Organizations, foundations and associations;

i)   Real estate activities, and of purchase and sale of real estate property;

j)   Investment services;

k)   Political parties, citizen groups and indigenous communities;

l)   Activities related to movements of money susceptible of being used for money laundering and other financial, economic and commercial activities established in the Code of Commerce.

II.   The entities or subjects mentioned in the aforementioned section shall report sua sponte to the Financial Investigations Unit when, while in exercise of their functions and/or activities, they detect the possible commission of corruption acts or crimes.

ARTICLE 22. (Management of Information).

I.   The information obtained by the Financial Investigations Unit, can neither be shared nor published during the analysis and investigation phase.

II.   When the Financial Investigations Unit considers that the information contains alleged acts of corruption, it will remit it along with all of its supporting documents to the Public Ministry and will make it known to the Attorney General of the State.

III.   The information analyzed by the Public Ministry, can be presented as evidence within penal processes.

ARTICLE 23. (Integrated System of Anti-Corruption Information and Recovery of State Property)

I.   The Integrated System of Anti-Corruption Information and Recovery of State Property – SIIARBE [Acronym in Spanish] is created, in charge of the Ministry of Institutional Transparency and Fight Against Corruption. The same has as its objective the centralization and exchange of information of the entities related with the fight against corruption, to design and apply preventive, repressive and sanctionatory policies and strategies, as well as to conduct the efficient follow-up and monitoring of the processes found within the scope of the fight against corruption.

II.   The SIIARBE will have within its attributions the verification sua sponte of the sworn declarations of assets and incomes of those public servants classified in accordance to indicators, parameters and criteria defined by the entities related with the fight against corruption.

III.   A Supreme Decree will establish its scope, internal obligations, attributions and procedures to be applied.

CHAPTER III

CORRUPTION CRIMES

ARTICLE 24. (Systematization of Corruption and Linked Crimes). Aside from those defined in the Chapter herein, the following Articles of the Penal Code are considered corruption crimes: 142, 144, 145, 146, 147, 149, 150, 151, 152, second paragraph of Articles 153 and 154, 157, 158, 172 bis, fourth paragraph of Article 173, 173 bis, 174, 221, first paragraph of Article 222 and 224, second paragraph of Article 225.

The following Articles included in the Penal Code are considered crimes linked to corruption: 132, 132 bis, 143, 150 bis, 153, 154, 177, 185 bis, 228, 228 bis, 229 and 230.

ARTICLE 25. (Creation of New Types of Penal Offences). The following types of penal offences are created:

1)   Undue use of public property or services;
2)   Illicit enrichment;
3)   Illicit enrichment by individuals that affects the State;
4)   Favoring illicit enrichment;
5)   Transnational active bribery;
6)   Transnational passive bribery;
7)   Obstruction of justice; and
8)   Falseness of the sworn declaration of assets and income.

ARTICLE 26. (Undue Use of Public Property or Services). The public servant that for its own benefit, or the benefit of a third individual, gives a different use to properties, rights and shares that belong to the State or its institutions, to which it has access due to the exercise of the public function, will be sanctioned with imprisonment of one to four years.

If as a result of the undue use, the property suffers deterioration, damage or perishes, the sanction will be of three to eight years plus the reparation of the damage caused.

The sanction of the first paragraph will be applied to the individual or public servant that uses the services of persons compensated by the State or of persons that are complying with a legal duty, giving them a different end than the one they were originally hired or destined for.

ARTICLE 27. (Illicit Enrichment). The public servant that has disproportionately increased its patrimony with regards to its legitimate earnings without providing a justification, will be sanctioned with imprisonment from five to ten years, disqualification for the exercise of the public functions and/or elected posts, a penalty of two hundred to five hundred days and the confiscation of the properties obtained illegally.

ARTICLE 28. (Illicit Enrichment by Individuals that Affects the State). The natural person that through a private activity has disproportionately increased its patrimony with regards to its legitimate earnings affecting the patrimony of the State, without being able of proving the situation otherwise, will be sanctioned with imprisonment from three to eight years, penalty of one hundred to three hundred days and the confiscation of the properties obtained illegally.

Will incur in the same crime and sanction, the legal representatives or ex representatives of juridical persons that through a private activity would have disproportionately increased the patrimony of the juridical person, affecting the patrimony of the State, without being able to prove that the origin thereof is a licit activity; also, the juridical person will restitute to the State the affected properties and will be sanctioned with a penalty of 25% of its patrimony.

ARTICLE 29. (Favoring Illicit Enrichment). The individual that provides his or her name or that participates in economic, financial and commercial activities with the goal of concealing, disguising or legitimating the increase in patrimony mentioned in the aforementioned articles, will be sanctioned with imprisonment from three to eight years, disqualification for the exercise of the public functions and/or elected posts and a penalty of fifty to five hundred days.

ESSENTIAL LAWS OF THE BOLIVIAN REVOLUTION

ARTICLE 30. (Transnational Active Bribery). The individual who promises, offers or grants in a direct or indirect manner, to a foreign public official, or from a public international organization, benefits or gifts, favors or advantages, that result in their own benefit or the benefit of another person or entity, with the goal of having such official act or refrain from acting while in exercise of its functions in order to obtain or maintain an undue benefit in relation to the conduction of international commercial activities, will be sanctioned with imprisonment from five to ten years and penalty of one hundred to five hundred days.

ARTICLE 31. (Transnational Passive Bribery). The foreign public official or official of an international public organization that requests or accepts in a direct or indirect manner an undue benefit that results in its own benefit or the benefit of another person or entity with the goal of having such official act or refrain from acting while in exercise of its functions, will be sanctioned with imprisonment of three to eight years and penalty of fifty to five hundred days.

ARTICLE 32. (Obstruction of Justice). The individual who uses physical strength, threats, intimidation, promises, offers or the granting of an undue benefit in order to induce a person to render false testimony or to hinder the giving of a testimony or the provision of evidence in processes of corruption crimes, will be sanctioned with imprisonment from three to eight years and penalty of thirty to five hundred says.

The sanction will be aggravated in one half for those who use physical strength, threats or intimidation in order to hinder the compliance of the official functions of judges, prosecutors, police members and other officials responsible of fighting against corruption.

ARTICLE 33. (Falseness of the Sworn Declaration of Assets and Incomes). The person who provides false, or omits to include, economic, financial and patrimonial details in the sworn declaration of assets and incomes, will incur in imprisonment from one to four years and penalty of fifty to two hundred days.

ARTICLE 34. (Modifications and Incorporations to the Penal Code). Articles 105, 142, 144, 145, 146, 147, 149, 150, 151, 152, 153, 154, 157, 173, 173 Bis, 174, 177, 185 Bis, 221, 222, 224, 225, 228, 229 and 230 are modified, and Articles 150 Bis, 172 Bis and 228 Bis are incorporated, in accordance to the following text:

ARTICLE 105. (Time Periods for the Prescription of the Penalty). The power to execute the penalty prescribes:

1)   In ten years, if it deals with a penalty of imprisonment

that is greater than six years.

2) In seven years, if it deals with penalties of imprisonment of less than six years and greater than two.

3) In five years, if it deals with the rest of the penalties.

These time periods will begin from the day of the notification with the sentence of conviction, or from the infringement of the sentence, if it had begun to be fulfilled.

The prescription of the penalty will not proceed, under any circumstance, in crimes of corruption.

ARTICLE 142. (Peculation). The public servant who, by taking advantage of the position being held, appropriates money, valuables or properties of which administration, collection or custody it is responsible, will be sanctioned with imprisonment from five to ten years and a fine of two hundred to five hundred days.

ARTICLE 144. (Embezzlement). The public servant, who gives a different application to the resources that it oversees, manages or perceives than the one they were intended for, will be sanctioned with imprisonment of three to eight years and a fine of one hundred to two hundred and fifty days.

If the act results in a damage or obstruction to public services, the penalty shall be increased by one third.

ARTICLE 145. (Individual Passive Bribery). The public servant or authority that in order to do or abstain from doing an act relating to its functions or contrary to the duties of its office, receives directly or through another person, for himself or herself or a third party, gifts or any other advantage or accepts offers or promises, shall be punished with imprisonment of three to eight years and a fine from fifty to one hundred fifty days.

ARTICLE 146. (Undue Use of Influences). The public servant or authority that directly or through another person and taking advantage of the functions performed, or by misusing the influences arising therefrom obtains advantages or benefits for himself or herself or a third party, shall be punished with imprisonment of three to eight years and a fine of one hundred to five hundred days.

ARTICLE 147. (Benefits By Reason of the Position Held). The public servant or authority that by reason of its position admits gifts or other benefits, shall be punished with imprisonment of three to eight years and a fine of one hundred to two hundred and fifty days.

ARTICLE 147. (Omission of the Declaration of Assets and Income). The public servant that according to the Law is bound to declare its assets and incomes at the time of taking possession or leaving office and does not do it, shall be punished with a fine of thirty days.

ARTICLE 150. (Negotiations Incompatible with the Exercise of Public Functions). The public servant who by itself or through another person or through a simulated act gets involved and obtains for itself or for a third person a benefit in any contract, supply, auction or operation involved by reason of its office, shall be punished with imprisonment of five to ten years and a fine of thirty to five hundred days.

ARTICLE 150 Bis. (Negotiations Incompatible with the Exercise of Public Functions by Individuals). The offense set forth in the preceding article shall also be applied to the arbitrators, experts, auditors, accountants, and auctioneers, and other professionals with regards to acts in which they, by virtue of their office, are involved and to the tutors, curators, executors and trustees regarding the property belonging to their wards, cured, wills, contests, assessments and similar acts, with imprisonment of five to ten years and a fine of thirty to five hundred days.

ARTICLE 151. (Extortion). The public servant or authority that with abuse of its status or function, directly or indirectly, requires or obtains money or other improper advantage or a higher proportion than the legally set, for its benefit or the benefit of a third party, shall be punished with imprisonment from three to eight years.

ARTICLE 152. (Exactions). The public servant who requires or obtains the exactions stated in the previous article to convert them in benefit of the public administration, shall be punished with imprisonment of one to four years.

If any kind of violence is used in the cases of the previous articles, the penalty shall be increased by one third.

ARTICLE 153. (Resolutions Contrary to the Constitution and the Laws). The public servant or authority that dictates resolutions or orders that contravene the Constitution or the laws, or implements or makes enforcement of such decisions or orders shall be punished with imprisonment from five to ten years.

The same penalty, will be applied when the resolution is issued by a prosecutor.

If the offence causes economic damage to the State, the penalty shall be increased by one third.

ARTICLE 154. (Breach of Duties). The public servant, who illegally omits, refuses or delays an act that is typical of its duties, shall be punished with imprisonment of one to four years.

The penalty shall be increased by one third, when the offence causes economic damage to the State.

ARTICLE 157. (Illegal Appointments). The public servant who proposes for a list, or appoints for public office, a person that does not satisfy the legal conditions for the specific position, shall be punished with imprisonment of one to four years and a fine of thirty to one hundred days.

ARTICLE 172 Bis. (Receivables Coming from Corruption Crimes). The person that, after a crime of corruption has been committed, helps the author to assure the benefit or result thereof or receives, conceals, sells or acquires the proceeds of the crime, shall be punished with imprisonment of three to eight years and the forfeiture of the unlawfully obtained assets.

ARTICLE 173. (Prevarication). The judge that while in exercise of its functions renders decisions that are manifestly contrary to the Law, shall be punished with imprisonment from five to ten years.

If as a result of the prevarication during criminal proceedings an innocent person is condemned, a more severe penalty than the lawful one is applied or an illegal preventive detention is imposed, the penalty established in the previous paragraph shall be increased by one third.

The arbitrators or amicable conciliators, or those who render analog functions of making decisions or issuing resolutions, who commit this crime, shall be penalized with imprisonment of three to eight years.

If a damage to the State is caused the penalty shall be increased by one third.

ARTICLE 173 Bis. (Passive Bribery by a Judge or Prosecutor). The judge or prosecutor who accepts pledges or gifts to make, take or omit to make an order or decision concerning the matters under its jurisdiction, shall be punished with imprisonment from five to ten years and a fine of two hundred to five hundred days, plus the disqualification to access to any public and/or elected office function.

The same penalty shall be imposed over the attorneys that with the same purpose and effect, procure such consortium with one or more judges or prosecutors, or who participate with them.

ARTICLE 174. (Consortium of Judges, Prosecutors and/or Attorneys). The judge or prosecutor who procures the formation of consortiums with one or more attorneys, or that participates with them, in order to procure illicit economic advantages in detriment of the sound administration of justice, shall be punished with imprisonment of five to ten years.

ARTICLE 177. (Negative or Retardation of Justice). The judicial or administrative official that while in exercise of the public function with jurisdiction and competence, while administering justice, delays or fails to comply with the terms over which it decides with regards to procedures, arrangements, resolutions or decisions under procedural law, equality and justice and the prompt administration thereof, shall be punished with imprisonment from five to ten years.

ARTICLE 185 Bis. (Legitimization of Illegal Earnings). The person who acquires, converts or transfers property, resources or rights connected with crimes of: processing, trafficking of controlled substances, smuggling, corruption, organized crime, delinquent associations, trade and human trafficking, human organ trafficking, weapons trafficking and terrorism, in order to conceal or disguise the nature, origin, location, destination, movement or ownership thereof, shall be punished with imprisonment of five to ten years, disqualification from public office and/or elected posts and a fine of two hundred to five hundred days.

This offense will also apply to the conduct described above even though the crimes of which the illicit proceeds come from have been committed wholly or partly in another country, provided that such acts are considered criminal in both countries.

The person who facilitates or encourages the commission of this crime shall be punished with imprisonment of four to eight years.

It is confirmed that the crime of legitimization of illicit proceeds is autonomous and will be investigated, tried and sentenced without previous conviction, regarding the crimes mentioned in the first paragraph.

ARTICLE 221. (Damaging Contracts for the State). The public servant, who knowingly enters into contracts that are detrimental for the State or for the autonomous, autarkic, mixed or decentralized entities, shall be punished with imprisonment from five to ten years.

If case of acting negligently, the punishment shall be imprisonment of one to four years.

The individual that in the same conditions as before enters into a contract that is harmful to the national economy shall be punished with imprisonment of three to eight years.

ARTICLE 222. (Breach of Contracts). The person who after having entered into contracts with the State or with the entities referred to in the previous article, does not comply without just cause, shall be punished with imprisonment of three to eight years.

If the breach results in the guilt of the obliged party, it shall be punished with imprisonment of one to four years.

ARTICLE 224. (Anti-Economic Conduct). The public servant or the person that, while in exercise of managerial functions or others of responsibility in institutions or enterprises of the State, causes due to mismanagement, poor technical direction or any other cause, damages to the property or the interests of the State, shall be punished with imprisonment of three to eight years.

If acting negligently, it will be sanctioned with imprisonment of one to four years.

ARTICLE 225. (Economic Disloyalty). The public servant or the person that because of its position or duties shall be found in possession of data or information that must be kept in reserve, regarding economic policy and reveals it, shall be punished with imprisonment of one to four years.

The same penalty increased by one third will be applied to the public servant or the person who in the above conditions has used or revealed such information or news for its own benefit or the benefit of another.

If acting negligently, the penalty will be decreased by one third.

ARTICLE 228. (Illegal Contributions and Advantages). The person who by abusing his or her official status or by simulating functions, representations, instructions or superior orders, by itself or through another person, requires, or obtains money or other economic advantage for personal gain or the gain of a third party, shall be penalized with imprisonment of one to three years.

If the author is a public servant, the penalty shall be increased by a third.

ARTICLE 228 Bis. (Illegal Contributions and Advantages of the Public Servant). If the conduct described in the previous article was committed by a public servant, causing economic damage to the State, the penalty shall be of imprisonment of three to eight years.

ARTICLE 229. (Fictitious Partnerships or Associations). Whoever organizes or directs companies, cooperatives or other fictitious associations to get by these means improper benefits or privileges, will be punished with imprisonment of one to four years and a fine of one hundred to five hundred days.

If it is a public servant who by himself or herself or through another person commits the crime, the punishment applied will be of imprisonment of three to eight years and a fine of thirty to one hundred days.

ARTICLE 230. (Illegal Franchises, Releases or Privileges). The person, who illegally secures, negotiates or uses releases, franchises, privileges, diplomatic or otherwise, shall be punished with imprisonment of three to eight years.

The public servant that illegally provides, uses or negotiates such releases, franchises or privileges, shall be punished with the penalty established in the preceding paragraph, increased by one third.

ARTICLE 35. (Voluntary Report). The person who has participated or participates as an instigator, accomplice or accessory, and who voluntarily reports and assists in the investigation and prosecution of the crimes codified in Articles 24 and 25 of this Law, will benefit from the reduction of two thirds of the corresponding sentence.

CHAPTER IV

INCLUSIONS AND AMENDMENTS TO THE CRIMINAL PROCEDURE CODE, CIVIL CODE AND ORGANIC LAW OF THE ATTORNEY GENERAL

ARTICLE 36. (Inclusion of Articles to the Criminal Procedure Code). Hereby be included to the Criminal Procedure Code, articles 29 Bis, 91 Bis, 148 Bis, 253 Bis and 344 Bis, in accordance to the following Text:

ARTICLE 29 Bis. (Imprescriptibility). In accordance to Article 112 of the Political Constitution of the State, the crimes committed by public servants who violate the patrimony of the State and cause severe economic damage, are imprescribable and do not admit the regime of immunity.

ARTICLE 91 Bis. (Continuation of the Trial in Absentia). When a defendant is declared a rebel due to its non-appearance in criminal proceedings for the crimes established in Articles 24, 25 et seq. of the Law Against Corruption, Illicit Enrichment and Investigation of Fortunes, the process will not be suspended with regards to the rebel. The State shall appoint a public defender and the accused will be tried in absentia, along with the other defendants present.

ARTICLE 148 Bis. (Asset Recovery Abroad). The State can request foreign authorities for the effective cooperation necessary to recover property and assets stolen by public servants and former public servants, which are object or product of crimes of corruption and related offenses found outside the country.

ARTICLE 253 Bis. (Process of Seizure within Crimes of Corruption). In case of crimes of corruption that cause serious damage to the State, since the beginning of the investigations and prior to a prosecutor request to the jurisdictional and competent authority within a deadline of five days, the process of seizure of the property and assets reasonably presumed to be the medium, instrument or result of the crime will begin, with full inventory in the presence of a Notary Public, designating a depositary in accordance with the Law, and when completing the formalities of the case the court shall decide, in sentencing, the confiscation of such property and assets in favor of the State if applicable.

ARTICLE 344 Bis. (Procedure for Trial in Absentia for Crimes of Corruption.) In case of proving the non-appearance of the accused within crimes of corruption, he or she will be declared a rebel and a new hearing trial day will be set for its conclusion in his or her absence, with the participation of its public defender, in this case, notifying the rebel with the resolutions through edicts.

ARTICLE 37. (Modifications to the Criminal Procedure Code). Articles 90, 366 and 368 of the Criminal Procedure Code are modified, in accordance to the following text:

ARTICLE 90. (Effects of Being Declared a Rebel). The declaration of rebel does not suspend the preparation phase. When declared during the trial, it is suspended over the rebel and will continue for the other defendants present, except in crimes of corruption, having to continue the criminal proceedings against all the accused, present or not.

The declaration of rebel interrupts the prescription.

ARTICLE 366. (Conditional Suspension of the Sentence). The judge or the court, after the necessary reports and taking into account the motives or causes that have led to the crime, the nature and modality of the fact, may conditionally suspend the execution of the sentence when the following requirements come together:

1)That the person has been sentenced to imprisonment for a period that does not exceed three years; 2) The person has not been the subject of previous conviction of a felony, within the last five years.

The conditional suspension of the sentence does not apply in crimes of corruption.

ARTICLE 368. (Judicial Pardon). The judge or court when dictating a conviction sentence, will grant judicial pardon for the author or participant that for a first offense has been sentenced to imprisonment not exceeding two years.

The judicial pardon will not proceed, under any circumstance, in crimes of corruption.

ARTICLE 38. (Regime Applicable to the Investigation). The crimes of corruption will be governed in their procedure of investigation and judgment by what is established in the Penal Procedure Code, in all of what does not contravene what is set forth in this Law.

ARTICLE 39. (Modifications to the Civil Code). Articles 1502, 1552 and 1553 of the Civil Code are modified, in accordance to the following text:

ARTICLE 1502. (Exceptions). The prescription does not proceed:

1) Against the person who resides or is found outside the national territory while in service for the State, until thirty days after having ceased in its functions.

2) Against the creditor of an obligation subjected to a condition or fixed day, until the condition is fulfilled or the day arrives.

3) Against the heir with benefit of inventory, regarding the credits it has against the succession.

4) Between spouses.

5) Regarding an action of guarantee, until the eviction happens.

6) With regards to the debts for economic damages to the State.

7) In the other cases established by law.

ARTICLE 1552. (Preventive Filing in the Registry).

I. The persons who can request the jurisdictional authority the preventive filing of its rights in the public registry:

1) Those that demand in a trial of real estate property, or that constitute, declares, modify or extinguish any real right.

2) Those that obtain in their favor an affidavit of attachment or a writ of attachment executed over the real estate property of the debtor.

3) Those that in any trial obtain a sentence passed in authority of a judged cause by which the defendant is ordered to comply with an obligation.

4) Those that present a claim to obtain a sentence concerning impediments or prohibitions that limit or restrict the free disposition of the properties, in accordance to Article 1540 numeral 14).

5) Those that have a title of which definitive registration cannot be

conducted due to the lack of any amendable requirement.

6)   The Attorney General of the State and the Ministry of Institutional Transparency and Fight Against Corruption, for the effects of the protection of the Patrimony of the State.

II.   In the cases foreseen by the article herein and when it concerns the movable properties subjected to registration, the filing will be practiced in the corresponding registries.

ARTICLE 1553. (Term of the Preventive Filing).

I.   The preventive filing will expire if on the second year after its date it is not converted to a registration. The judge can extend the term for a new lapse of one year, which will not be detrimental for the third if it is not seated at the same time in the registry.

II.   The preventive filing will be converted to registration when the sentence passed in authority of a judged cause is presented, or demonstrating to have rectified the cause that hindered momentarily the registration and the same in these cases produces all of its effects since the date of the filing, aside from any right registered in the interval.

III.   The preventive filing in favor of the State will expire after four years, extendable to two more, if it is not converted into a definitive registration.

ARTICLE 40. (Inclusion in the Organic Law of the Public Ministry). It is included to numeral 36) of Article 36 of the Law N° 2175, the Organic Law of the Public Ministry, the following text:

36)   Appoint in each Department the prosecutors specialized and dedicated exclusively to the investigation and accusation of the crimes of corruption.

DEROGATORY DISPOSITION

Unique. The following norms are derogated:

a) Article 158 of the Law N° 1488 dated April 14th of 1993 (Law of Banks and Financial Entities, modified by Law N° 2297 dated December 20th of 2001 – Law of Strengthening of the Norms and Financial Supervision).

b) All legal dispositions contrary to the Law herein.

TRANSITORY DISPOSITIONS

First. Until the anti-corruption courts created by Article 11 of the Law herein are not found in functioning, the judges that take cognizance and process penal procedures will grant priority to the processing and resolution of the processes in which the interests of the State are at stake.

Second. The cases processed for crimes of corruption shall be known by the judges [feminine], the judges [masculine] and the tribunals, until the new anti-corruption courts are elected to be afterwards transferred to them.

FINAL DISPOSITIONS

First. The actions of investigation and judgment of permanent crimes of corruption and those linked thereto, established in Article 25 numerals 2) and 3) of the Law herein, must be applied by the competent authorities within the framework of Article 123 of the Political Constitution of the State.

The numerals 1), 4), 5), 6), 7) and 8) of Article 25, will be processed within the framework of Article 116, paragraph II of the Political Constitution of the State.

Second. (Of the Financing). The State will guarantee the annual financing of the policies and projects of the fight against corruption with its own resources, to guarantee the adequate margins of investigation, accusation and judgment.

Remit it to the Executive Organ, for constitutional purposes.

Is given in the Hall of Sessions of the Plurinational Legislative Assembly, on the twenty-ninth day of the month of march of the year two thousand and ten.

Signed. René Oscar Martínez Callahuanca, Héctor Enrique Arce Zaconeta, Andrés A. Villca Daza, Clementina Garnica Cruz, José Antonio Yucra Paredes, Pedro Nuny Caity.

As such, I enact it in order to have it and comply with it as a Law of the Plurinational State of Bolivia.

Palace of Government of the city of La Paz, March thirty-first of two thousand and ten.

SIGNED. EVO MORALES AYMA, Oscar Coca Antezana, Sacha Sergio Llorenty Soliz, Nilda Copa Condori, Nardi Suxo Iturry.

LAW AGAINST RACISM AND ANY FORM OF DISCRIMINATION

As published by the *Gaceta Oficial de Bolivia* on October 2010.

LAW N° 045
LAW OF OCTOBER 8th OF 2010

EVO MORALES AYMA
PRESIDENT OF THE PLURINATIONAL STATE OF BOLIVIA

For which, the Plurinational Legislative Assembly, has sanctioned the following Law:

THE PLURINATIONAL LEGISLATIVE ASSEMBLY

DECREES:

LAW AGAINST RACISM AND ANY FORM OF DISCRIMINATION

CHAPTER 1
GENERAL DISPOSITIONS

Article 1. (PURPOSE AND OBJECTIVES).

I.   The Law herein has the purpose of establishing the mechanisms and procedures for the prevention and sanction of acts of racism and any form of discrimination within the framework of the Political Constitution of the State and the International Treaties of Human Rights.

II.   The Law herein has as its objectives to eliminate the conducts of racism and any form of discrimination and to consolidate public policies of protection and prevention of crimes of racism and any form of discrimination.

Article 2. (GENERAL PRINCIPLES). The Law herein is governed by the principles of:

a)   Interculturality. Understood as the interaction among the cultures, constituting an instrument for the cohesion and the harmonious and balanced coexistence among all of the peoples and the nations for the construction of relations of equality and equity in a respectful manner.

b) **Equality.** All of the human beings are born free and equal in dignity and right. The State will promote the necessary conditions to achieve real and effective equality adopting measures and policies of affirmative and/or differentiated action that value diversity, with the objective of achieving equity and social justice, guaranteeing specific equitable conditions for the enjoyment and exercise of the rights, freedoms and guarantees that are recognized in the Political Constitution of the State, the national laws and the international norms of human rights.

c) **Equity.** Understood as the recognition to the difference and the equitable social value of the persons to achieve the social justice and the full exercise of the civil, political, economic, social and cultural rights.

d) **Protection.** All of the human beings have the right to equal protection against racism and any form of discrimination, in an effective and timely manner in the administrative and/or jurisdictional venues, which implies a just and adequate reparation or satisfaction for any damage suffered as a consequence and the racist and/or discriminatory act.

Article 3. (SCOPE AND FIELD OF APPLICATION). The Law herein will be applied in the entire national territory and in the places subjected to its jurisdiction.

It does not recognize any immunity, exception or privilege and it is applied:

a) To all of the Bolivians [masculine] and the Bolivians [feminine] of origin or nationalized and to every dweller and inhabitant in the national territory that is found under the jurisdiction of the State.

b) To the authorities, public servants and ex public servants of the Executive, Legislative, Judicial and Electoral organs of the Plurinational State of Bolivia, its entities and institutions of the central level, decentralized or deconcentrated and to the autonomous, departmental, municipal, regional and indigenous originary farmer territorial entities.

c) To the Public Ministry, the Attorney General of the State, the Public Defender, the Universities, the National Police, the Armed Forces and any entity of the structure of the State.

d)   To private juridical persons, to national or foreign non-governmental institutions through their representatives.

e)   To social organizations and mechanisms of social control.

f)   To bilateral, multilateral and special diplomatic missions exercising functions in the Bolivian territory, in accordance to the norms of international law.

Article 4. (OBSERVATION). The authorities of national, departmental, regional, municipal, indigenous originary farmer, or of any other hierarchy, will observe the Law herein, in accordance, with the Political Constitution of the State and the international norms and instruments concerning human rights, against racism and any form of discrimination, which are ratified by the Plurinational State of Bolivia.

Article 5.   (DEFINITIONS).   For the effects of application and interpretation of the Law herein, the following definitions are adopted:

a)   **Discrimination.** "Discrimination" is used to define any form of distinction, exclusion, restriction or preference founded over reason of sex, color, age, sexual orientation and identity of gender, origin, culture, nationality, citizenship, language, religious creed, ideology, political or philosophical affiliation, civil status, economic, social or health condition, profession, occupation or activity, level of instruction, different capabilities and/or physical, intellectual or sensorial disability, state of pregnancy, origin, physical appearance, clothing, surname or others that have as their objective or result the annulment or the undermining of the recognition, enjoyment and exercise, in conditions of equality, of the human rights and the fundamental freedoms recognized by the Political Constitution of the State and by international law. The measures of affirmative action are not considered discrimination.

b)   **Racial Discrimination.** It is understood as "racial discrimination" any distinction, exclusion, restriction or preference based in reasons of race or due to color, ancestry or national or ethnic origin that have as their objective or result in the direct or indirect annulment or the undermining of the recognition, enjoyment and exercise, in conditions of equality, of the human rights and the fundamental freedoms recognized by the Political Constitution of the State and by the international norms of Human Rights, in the political, economic, social, cultural or in any other sphere of the public and/or private life.

c)   **Racism.** It is considered as "racism" any theory tending to the valuation of some biological and/or cultural differences, real or imaginary in benefit of a group and in prejudice of another, with the goal of justifying an aggression and a system of domination that presumes the superiority of one group over another.

d)   **Race.** The "race" is a socially constructed notion, developed throughout history as a group of prejudices that distorts the ideas concerning the human differences and the group behavior. It is used to assign to some groups an inferior status and to others a superior status that grants them access to privilege, to power and to wealth. Any doctrine of superiority based on racial differentiation is scientifically false, morally condemnable, socially unjust and dangerous and nothing in theory or in practice allows justifying racial discrimination.

e)   **Equality of Gender.** It is the recognition and valuation of the physical and biological differences of women and men, with the goal of achieving a social justice and an equality of opportunities which guarantees the full benefit of their rights without prejudice to their sex within the areas of the social, economic, political, cultural and family life.

f)   **Generational Equality.** It is the recognition and valuation of the generational differences of women and men, with the goal of achieving a social justice which guarantees the full benefit of their rights without prejudice to their age within the areas of the social, economic, political, cultural and family life.

g)   **Homophobia.** It is referred to the aversion, hate, prejudice or discrimination against homosexual men or women, including also the rest of the persons that integrate the sexual diversity.

h)   **Transphobia.** It is understood as the discrimination against trans-sexuality and of transsexual or transgender persons, based in their identity of gender.

i) **Xenophobia.** It is understood as the hate and the rejection of a foreigner [masculine] and of a foreigner [feminine], with manifestations that go from a more or less manifested rejection, disdain and threats, to even aggressions and diverse forms of violence.

j) **Misogyny.** It is understood as misogyny and conduct or behavior of manifested hate against women or the female gender, independently of age, origin and/or level of instruction that achieves or pretends to violate directly or indirectly the Human Rights and the principles of the Law herein.

k) **Affirmative Action.** It is understood as affirmative action those measures and policies of temporary character adopted in favor of the sectors of the population in situation of disadvantage and who suffer discrimination in the exercise and effective enjoyment of the rights recognized in the Political Constitution of the State and in the international instruments. It constitutes an instrument to overcome the obstacles that hinder a real equality.

l) **Corrective Action.** The effective imposition of penalizing or disciplinary measures to the offenders, conducting the follow-up to their application and the results obtained.

CHAPTER II

OF THE MEASURES OF PREVENTION AND EDUCATION, DESTINED TO ERADICATE THE RACISM AND ANY FORM OF DISCRIMINATION

Article 6. (PREVENTION AND EDUCATION). It is the duty of the Plurinational State of Bolivia to define and adopt a public policy of prevention and fight against racism and any form of discrimination, with a gender and generational perspective, of application in all of the departmental and municipal national territorial levels, which contains the following actions:

I. **Within the educational sphere:**

a) To promote the design and implementation of institutional policies of prevention and fight against racism and discrimination within Universities, in public or private National Superior Teaching Institutes, and in the National

Educational System in the pre-school, primary and secondary levels.

b)   To design and initiate educational, cultural, communicational policies of intercultural dialogue, attacking the structural causes of racism and any form of discrimination; which recognize and respect the benefits of the diversity and the plurinationality and that include in their contents the history and the rights of the indigenous originary farmer nations and peoples and the afro-Bolivian communities.

c)   To promote the implementation of processes of formation and education in human rights and in values, within the programs of formal and non-formal education, appropriate for all the levels of the educational process, based in the principles stated in the Law herein, in order to modify attitudes and behaviors founded in racism and discrimination; to promote the respect for diversity; and counteract sexism, prejudice, stereotypes and all practices of racism and/or discrimination.

II.   **Within the public administration sphere.**

a)   To train the servants [feminine] and the servants [masculine] of the public administration concerning the measures of prevention, sanction and elimination of racism and any form of discrimination.

b)   To promote and support the curricular inclusion of the prevention against racism and discrimination in the Military and Police Institutes.

c)   To promote institutional policies of prevention and fight against racism and discrimination within the systems of education, health and others that include the rendering of public services.

d)   The adoption of procedures or protocols for the attention of specific populations.

e)   To promote functional ethics and good treatment in the attention of the citizenship.

f)   To guarantee that the political and juridical systems reflect the plurinationality of the Bolivian State within the framework of the Human Rights.

g)   To promote the recognition of the national heroes and the heroines belonging to the indigenous originary farmer nations and peoples, the afro-Bolivian people and the intercultural communities.

III. **Within the communication, information and dissemination sphere.**

a)   The State shall promote the production and dissemination of statistical data, concerning racism and any form of discrimination with the goal of eliminating the social inequalities.

b)   To promote the conduction of investigations and quantitative and qualitative studies, concerning racism and any form of discrimination, as well as the effects of these phenomena over its victims, with the goal of defining policies and programs aimed to combat them.

c)   The public and private communication mediums shall provide themselves with internal mechanisms to guarantee the elimination of racism and any form of discrimination, with regards to its responsibility to generate public opinion in accordance to the Political Constitution of the State.

d)   To arrange that the communication mediums, including radio, television, print and the new information and communication technologies, such as the internet, eliminate from the programming, racist, xenophobic, and other discriminatory content from their languages, expressions and manifestations.

e)   To disseminate the content of the Law herein; the national and international instruments against racism and any form of discrimination; and the public policies related to the topic.

f)   The communication mediums shall support the measures and actions against racism and any form of discrimination.

IV.   **Within the economic sphere.**

   a)   The State shall promote the social inclusion through the execution of the public and private investments to generate opportunities and the eradication of poverty; aimed specially to the most vulnerable sectors.

CHAPTER III

OF THE NATIONAL COMMITTEE AGAINST RACISM AND ANY FORM OF DISCRIMINATION

   Article 7. (COMMITTEE). The National Committee against Racism and Any Form of Discrimination is created, which is in charge of promoting, designing and implementing integral policies and norms against racism and any form of discrimination.

   The National Committee against Racism and Any Form of Discrimination will be under the tuition of the Ministry of Cultures through the Vice-Ministry of Decolonization.

   The Committee will be formed by two commissions:

   a)   Commission for the Fight against Racism

   b)   Commission for the Fight against Any Form of Discrimination.

   The functioning of both commissions will be at the charge of the General Direction for the Fight Against Racism and any form of Discrimination, of the Vice-Ministry of Decolonization, dependent of the Ministry of Cultures.

   Article 8.   (MEMBERS OF THE COMMITTEE AGAINST RACISM AND ANY FORM OF DISCRIMINATION).

I.   For the effects of this Law, the Committee against Racism and any form of Discrimination will be formed by the:

   a)   Public institutions: 1. The Executive Organ: Ministry of Cultures, Ministry of the Presidency, Ministry of Justice, Ministry of Government, Ministry of Education, Ministry of Economy and Public Finances, Ministry of Planning for Development and Ministry of Defense; 2. The Judicial Organ; 3. The Electoral Organ; 4. The Legislative Organ:

Commission of Human Rights of the Chamber of Deputies; 5. The Departmental Autonomous Governments; 6. The Municipal Autonomous Governments; 7. The Indigenous Originary Farmer Autonomies.

b)   Social Organizations.

c)   Indigenous Originary Farmer Organizations.

d)   Intercultural Communities and Afro-Bolivian Communities.

e)   Organizations that defend the rights of the women, the youth, the children and the adolescents, the persons with disabilities and the vulnerable sectors of the society.

f)   Other institutions and/or organizations that defend the Human Rights and the civil society.

II.   The Office of the High Commissionaire for Human Rights of Bolivia and the Public Defender as observing and technological company organs.

III.   The members of the Committee, for these functions, will not perceive any salary coming from the General Treasury of the Nation.

IV.   The Vice-Ministry of Decolonization can hire technical, professional or non-professional personnel, to support the functioning of the National Committee against Racism and any form of Discrimination.

V.   The commissions: a) for the fight against racism and b) for the fight against any form of discrimination, will be formed by the delegates of the committees, in accordance to an internal regulation.

Article 9. (OF THE FUNCTIONS OF THE COMMITTEE). The Committee against Racism and any form of Discrimination will have as its main duties:

a)   To direct the preparation of a Diagnosis and a National Plan of Action against Racism and any Form of Discrimination, concerning the base of the guidelines proposed in Article 6 of the Law herein.

b)   To promote, develop and implement public policies of prevention and for the fight against racism and any form of discrimination.

c)   To oversee the respect for equality and non-discrimination in the proposals for public policies and projects of law.

d)   To conduct the follow-up, evaluation and monitoring of the implementation of the public policies and the norms in effect against racism and any form of discrimination.

e)   To see to that the Internal Personnel Regulations, the Disciplinary regulations and others within the Public Administration, the Bolivian Police and the Armed Forces, include as a cause for an internal proceeding, faults relative to racism and any form of discrimination, in accordance to the Law herein.

f)   To promote in all of the public entities, the creation of instances of prevention against racism and any form of discrimination, as well as the reception of the denunciations and the promotion of administrative proceedings until their conclusion, in accordance to the regulation.

g)   To promote the formation of Commissions and Committees against Racism and any form of Discrimination, with the purpose of implementing prevention measures within the framework of the autonomies.

h)   To promote the public recognition of the natural and /or juridical persons of the State or of the private sector who have shined for their labor against racial discrimination or any form of discrimination.

i)   To promote the recognition of the Bolivian heroes and the Bolivian heroines, belonging to the indigenous originary farmer nations and peoples, the Afro-Bolivian people and of intercultural communities.

Article 10. (REGISTRATION AND FOLLOW-UP OF THE ADMINISTRATIVE AND JUDICIAL PROCESSES FOR RACISM AND ANY FORM OF DISCRIMINATION). With the purpose of registration and follow-up, the National Committee Against Racism and any form of Discrimination; the Ministry of Cultures through the Vice-Ministry of Decolonization, will systematize and produce information concerning the administrative and judicial processes initiated due to a cause of racism and any form of discrimination.

Article 11. (BUDGET). The General Treasury of the Nation, will grant the economic resources necessary in an annual manner, to the Ministry of Cultures for the compliance of the functions stated in the Law herein.

CHAPTER IV

COMPETENT INSTANCES OF PROTECTION FOR THE VICTIMS OF RACISM AND ANY FORM OF DISCRIMINATION

Article 12. (COMPETENT INSTANCES). The persons that have suffered acts of racism or discrimination can opt for a constitutional, administrative or disciplinary and/or penal proceeding, as may correspond.

Article 13. (ADMINISTRATIVE OR DISCIPLINARY PROCEEDING IN PUBLIC INSTITUTIONS).

I.   The following conducts constitute faults while in exercise of the public function:

      a)   Verbal aggressions founded in racist and/or discriminatory reasons,

      b)   Refusal of access to service due to racist and/or discriminatory reasons.

      c)   Physical, psychological and sexual abuse due to racist and discriminatory reasons, which do not constitute a crime.
As long as these faults are committed while in exercise of their functions, within the relation among co-workers or with the users of the service.

II.   The racist and/or discriminatory reasons to which the preceding paragraph refers to, are found described in the Article 281 Bis and 281 Ter of the Penal Code.

III.   The public institution can order that the servant [feminine] or the servant [masculine], offender be subjected to psychological treatment, with the expenses being at the charge of the same institution.

IV.   All of the public institutions shall modify their Internal Personnel Regulations, their Disciplinary Regulations and others that correspond, in a manner to include the faults described in paragraph I of the Article herein, as a cause for the initiation of an internal process and reason for the administrative or disciplinary sanction.

V.   In case that in the administrative or internal process, it is determined the existence of penal responsibility, the public institution shall remit the case to the Public Ministry.

VI.   The acts of racism and any form of discrimination that constitute faults committed by public servants [feminine] or servants [masculine] will be denunciated to the same institution to which they belong to, in order to apply the corresponding administrative or disciplinary sanctions.

VII.   The public institution that takes cognizance of the denunciations concerning racism and any form of discrimination shall remit copy thereof to the General Direction for the Fight Against Racism and any form of Discrimination of the Vice-Ministry of Decolonization, of the Ministry of Cultures, for the purposes of registration and follow-up.

VIII.   The denouncing party, can remit copy of the denunciation against the public servant [feminine] or servant [masculine], to the Ministry of Cultures for the purposes of registration and follow-up.

Article 14. (PRIVATE INSTITUTIONS).

I.   All of the private institutions must adopt or modify their Internal Regulations in a manner to include as faults, racist and/or discriminatory conducts, such as:

   a)   Verbal aggressions for racist and/or discriminatory reasons,

   b)   Refusal of access to service for racist and/or discriminatory reasons,

   c)   Physical, psychological and sexual abuse for racist and/or discriminatory reasons, which does not constitute a crime,

   d)   Degrading actions.

II.   The racist and/or discriminatory reasons referred to by the preceding paragraph, are found described in the Article 281 Bis and 281 Ter of the Penal Code.

III.   In case of existing evidence of penal responsibility, it shall be remitted to the cognizance of the Public Ministry.

IV.   The private institution that takes cognizance of the denunciations concerning racism and any form of discrimination against its employees, shall remit copy them to the General Direction for the Fight Against Racism and Any Form of Discrimination of the Vice-Ministry of

Decolonization, of the Ministry of Cultures, for purposes of registration and follow-up.

Article 15. (PROHIBITION OF RESTRICTING THE ACCESS TO PUBLIC ESTABLISHMENTS)

I.   Any restriction of entrance and placing of signs with this purpose to premises or establishments of attention, service or entertainment that are open for the public, is prohibited, under sanction of closure during three days the first time, of thirty days the second time and definitively on the third. Except for those prohibitions set forth by the law that protect rights or for the activities that are not directed to the general public due to its content.

II.   This measure will be applied by the Municipal Autonomous Governments in accordance to a special regulation, who shall verify the extremes of the denunciation.

III.   It is declared mandatory to exhibit signs at the entrances of the public and private establishments of attention, service or entertainment open for the public, in a visible manner displaying the following text: "All persons are equal before the Law". In case of illegally restricting the access to public establishments, you can present your denunciation before the Municipal Autonomous Governments.

Article 16. (MASS MEDIUMS OF COMMUNICATION). The medium of communication that would authorize and publish racist and discriminatory ideas will be liable to receive economic sanctions and the suspension of the license for functioning, in accordance to regulation.

Article 17. (OBLIGATION OF DENOUNCING). The person that while in exercise of the public function shall take cognizance of events of racism and any form of discrimination, is in the obligation of denouncing it before the corresponding authorities; in case of not doing so will be liable to receive the sanction set forth in Article 178 of the Penal Code.

Article 18. (PROTECTION OF VICTIMS, WITNESSES AND DENUNCIATORS). The State guarantees the physical and psychological security of the victims, witnesses and denunciators of crimes of racism and any form of discrimination.

Article 19. (ALTERNATIVE MEASURES). In accordance to what is established by Article 26 of the Penal Procedure Code, the Public Ministry shall look within the framework of legality for the solution of the penal conflict, by means of the application of the alternative measures set forth by the law.

Article 20. (FALSE OR RECKLESS DENUNCIATION). The person that knowingly would accuse or denounce a person as the author [masculine] or the author [feminine], or participant of a crime of racism or any form of discrimination without having committed it, giving place to the initiation of the corresponding penal process, will be sanctioned in accordance to what is set forth in Article 166 of the Penal Code.

CHAPTER V

CRIMES AGAINST THE DIGNITY OF THE HUMAN BEING

Article 21. (CRIMES). The following disposition is included in Chapter II, of Title III of the First Book of the Penal Code:

"Article 40 Bis.- (General Aggravating Factor). The penalties of all crimes typified in the Special Part of this Code and in the other complementary penal laws will be elevated by one third the minimum and in one half the maximum, when they have been committed for the racist and/or discriminatory reasons set forth in Articles 281 bis and 281 ter of this same Code. In no case the penalty can exceed the maximum established by the Political Constitution of the State."

Article 22. Title VIII of the Second Book of the Penal Code is modified with the following text:

"Crimes Against the Life, the Integrity and the Dignity of the Human Being".

Article 23. It is incorporated to Title VIII of the Second Book of the Penal Code, the **"Chapter V"** called: **"Crimes against the Dignity of the Human Being"**, the same that shall contain the following dispositions:

Article 281 bis.- (Racism).

I. *A person who arbitrarily or illegally restricts, prevents, infringes upon, or impedes the exercise of individual or collective rights, motivated by race, national origin or ethnicity, color, ancestry, or for use of dress or language of, or for belonging to, nations or groups of indigenous originary farmers or of the Afro-Bolivian peoples, will be sanctioned to a prison sentence between three and seven years.*

II.   *The sanction will be aggravated at least by one third the minimum and by one half the maximum when:*

    a)   The act is committed by a public servant [masculine] or servant [feminine] or public authority.

    b)   The act is committed by an individual while rendering a public service.

    c)   The act is committed with violence.

Article 281 ter.- (Discrimination).

A person who arbitrarily or illegally obstructs, restricts, infringes upon, impedes or prevents the exercise of individual or collective rights, motivated by sex, age, gender, sexual orientation or gender identity, cultural identity, family affiliation, nationality, citizenship, language, religious creed, ideology, political opinion or philosophy, marital status, economic or social situation, illness, occupation, level of education, different capabilities or having a physical, intellectual or sensory disability, pregnancy, regional origin, physical appearance and dress, will be sanctioned with imprisonment of one to five years.

I.   *The sanction will be aggravated by one third the minimum and by one half the maximum when:*

    a)   *The act is committed by a public servant [masculine] or servant [feminine] or public authority.*

    b)   *The act is committed by an individual while rendering a public service.*

    c)   *The act is committed with violence.*

Article 281 quater. (Dissemination and Incitement of Racism or Discrimination)

A person who by whatever means disseminates ideas based on racial superiority or hate or that promote and/or justify racism or any form of discrimination, for the reasons described in Articles 281 bis and 281 ter, or incites violence or persecution of individual or groups of people, motivated by racist or discriminatory reasons will be sanctioned with imprisonment of one to five years.

I.   The sanction will be aggravated by one third the minimum and by one half the maximum, when the act is committed by a public servant [masculine] or servant [feminine] or by a public authority.

II.   When the act is committed by a social communications worker [masculine] or worker [feminine] or the owner thereof, without being able to claim immunity or any other exemption.

Article 281 septieser. (Racist or Discriminatory Organizations or Associations)

The person who participates in an organization or association which promotes and/or justifies racism or discrimination as described in Articles 281 bis and 281 ter or incites hate, violence, or persecution of individuals or groups based on racist or discriminatory motives, will be sanctioned with imprisonment of one to four years.

The sanction will be aggravated by one third the minimum and by one half the maximum, when the act is committed by a public servant [masculine] or servant [feminine] or by a public authority.

Article 281 octies.- (Insults and other Verbal Aggressions Based on Racist or Discriminatory Reasons)

Any person who by whatever means expresses insults or verbal aggressions, based on racist or discriminatory reasons as described in Articles 281 bis and 281 ter, will be sanctioned to provision of labor from forty days to eighteen months, and a fine of forty to one hundred days.

I.   *If this crime was committed via print, manuscript, or through any medium of communication, the penalty will be aggravated by one third the minimum and by one half the maximum*

II.   *If the person accused of this crime retracts, before or by the time of the formal imputation, the penal action will be extinguished. A second retraction concerning the same act will not be admitted.*

III.   *The retraction must be made in the same medium, in the same conditions and scope by which the insult or verbal aggression was conducted, assuming the costs implied by this retraction.*

Article 24. (THE PENAL ACTION). Article 20 and 26 of Title II of the First Book of the Penal Procedure Code are modified in the following terms:

Article 20°.- (Crimes of private action). The following are crimes of private action: the writing of a check without funds, the defective writing of a check, the diversion of clientele, corruption of dependents, undue appropriation, abuse of trust, crimes against the honor, the destruction of own things in order to defraud, food and services fraud, the concealment of property or civil deception, dispossession, alteration of boundaries, disturbance of possession, simple damage and insults and other verbal aggressions due to racist or discriminatory reasons.

The rest of the crimes are of public action.

Article 26°.- (Conversion of actions). To the request of the victim, the public penal action can be converted to a private action in the following cases:

1.   When it is a crime that requires the instance of the party, except for the exceptions set forth in Article 17° of this Code;

2.   When they are crimes of patrimonial content or culpable crimes that do not result in death as long as there is not a gravely compromised public interest; and,

3.   When they are "Crimes against the Dignity of the Human Being" as long as there is not a gravely compromised public interest,

4.   When the rejection set forth in Article 304° or the application of the criteria of opportunity set forth in numeral 1) of Article 21° of this Code has been ordered and the victim or the accusing party has formulated an opposition.

In the cases set forth in numerals 1) and 2) the conversion will be authorized of the District Attorney or by whoever he or she delegates, an authorization that will be issued within three days after it was requested. In the case of numeral 3) the conversion will be authorized by the competent judge.

FINAL DISPOSITION

UNIQUE. It is entrusted to the Ministry of Justice, the preparation of an ordered text of the Penal Code, including the modifications incorporated in the Law herein.

ABROGATING DISPOSITION

UNIQUE. All of the dispositions contrary to the Law herein are abrogated.

Remit it to the Executive Organ, for constitutional purposes.

Is given in the Hall of Sessions of the Plurinational Legislative Assembly, on the eighth day of the month of October of two thousand and ten.

Signed. René Oscar Martínez Callahuanca, Héctor Enrique Arce Zaconeta, Andrés A. Villca Daza, Clementina Garnica Cruz, Pedro Nuny Caity, José Antonio Yucra Paredes.

As such, I enact it in order to have it and comply with it as a Law of the Plurinational State of Bolivia.

Palace of Government of the city of La Paz, on the eighth day of the month of October of two thousand and ten.

SIGNED. EVO MORALES AYMA, Oscar Coca Antezana, Sacha Sergio Llorentty Soliz, Walter Juvenal Delgadillo Terceros MINISTRY OF PUBLIC WORKS, SERVICES, AND HOUSING AND INTERIM OF DEVELOPMENT PLANNING, Antonia Rodríguez Medrano MINISTER OF PRODUCTIVE DEVELOPMENT AND PLURAL ECONOMY AND INTERIM OF ECONOMIC AND PUBLIC FINANCES, Roberto Iván Aguilar Gómez, Nilda Copa Condori, Elizabeth Arismendi Chumacero MINISTER OF LEGAL DEFENSE OF THE STATE AND INTERIM OF AUTONOMIES, Zulma Yugar Párraga.

ABOUT THE TRANSLATOR

Luis Francisco Valle Velasco: Born in La Paz, Bolivia on September 6th, 1976. Attorney at Law and Legal Freelance Translator since the year 2002. Certified translator by the **United States Embassy in Bolivia**. Educated in the United States with a Bachelor of Science degree in International Business from **King's College (www.kings.edu)** in Wilkes-Barre, Pennsylvania; and in La Paz, Bolivia, with a Bachelor of Laws from **Universidad Privada Boliviana (www.upb.edu)**.

Review the translator's resume on:

http://luisfvalle.TranslatorsCafe.com

Contact the translator at **luisfvalle@gmail.com** to comment about this publication or for any legal document translation project you may have.

www.ingramcontent.com/pod-product-compliance
Lightning Source LLC
Chambersburg PA
CBHW032006170526
45157CB00002B/563